The Anarchist Reforestation Show

The Anarchist Reforestation Show

James M. Wright

METAMORPHIC PRESS

Copyright © 2024 by James M. Wright
All rights reserved. No part of this book may be reproduced in any manner whatsoever without written permission except in the case of brief quotations embodied in critical articles and reviews.
First Printing, 2024
Metamorphic Press, Bath, Maine

CONTENTS

	DEDICATION	vii
	PERSPECTIVES FOR A WORKER'S MEMOIR	ix
1	What the Fuck?	1
2	The Means of Production	11
3	Crummy Life	21
4	Flotation Devices	27
5	Burnt Orange	35
6	Men, Mosquitoes, and Machines	45
7	Back to Work	53
8	A Society of Sorts	61
9	Capitalist Roadkill	71
10	A Brief Career in Espionage	79
11	Down the Marmot Hole	87
12	Under the Volcano	95
13	MARMCO	101

14 | Under the Volcano Redux 107

15 | A Field Guide to Marmots 117

16 | Myrtlewood and Mao 125

17 | The Yaak Attack 135

18 | Cedar Rat Trials 147

19 | Party of the Last Part 159

ACKNOWLEDGMENTS 165
BIBLIOGRAPHY 167
ABOUT THE AUTHOR 169

I dedicate these stories to my comrades in the trenches of the reforestation industry. No doubt they have their own versions.

PERSPECTIVES FOR A WORKER'S MEMOIR

Enkidu worked his words, saying to Gilgamesh: "My friend, we have turned the forest into wasteland."
Gilgamesh, Tablet V, translated by Sophus Helle

It was the first time that the world had seen the deleterious environmental effects produced when steam, steel, and business enterprise combined with capital, rising affluence, and increased demand. It was an experience that, regrettably, was going to be repeated in one form or another in many other forests of the world in the future.
Michael Williams, *Deforesting the Earth: From Prehistory to Global Crisis*

...in the Tongass National Forest in southeastern Alaska, 400-year-old hemlock, spruce, and cedar are sold to huge timber corporations for less than the price of a cheeseburger....
Derrick Jensen and George Draffan, *Strangely Like War: The Global Assault on Forests*

Labour is, first of all, a process between man and nature, a process by which man, through his own actions, mediates, regulates and controls the metabolism between himself and nature. He con-

fronts the materials of nature as a force of nature. He sets in motion the natural forces which belong to his own body, his arms, legs, head and hands, in order to appropriate the material of nature in a form adapted to his own needs. Through this movement he acts upon external nature and changes it, and in this way he simultaneously changes his own nature.

Karl Marx, *Capital*, translated by Ben Fowkes

On the hills he planted pine groves
Clumps of fir upon the hillocks;
All the heaths he sowed with heather
And the dells with undergrowth.
Planted birches in the hollows,
In the loose loam planted alders;
In the damps the chokecherry seeded,
Planted sallows in the marshes;
Rowans in the holy places,
Willows in the soggy soils;
Junipers upon the barrens,
Oaks along the river banks.
Then the trees began to grow,
All the slender saplings stretching;
Pine trees spread their bushy tops
And the spruces flower-crowned.

Elias Lonnrot, *Kalevala: Epic of the Finnish People*, translated by Eino Friberg

1

What the Fuck?

By 1974, the Vietnam War had worn thin on the American people. A decade of demonstrations, riots, and political turmoil had undermined social stability. It seemed that something was coming to an end; I didn't know what. I had my sympathies, but I wasn't part of it; I lived in the North Cascades with my girlfriend, a long way from the real world. My life had been desperate and monkish until I met her. She was tolerant of my ways, but I found that we needed things I'd learned to live without, like food and shelter. Sure, we lived rent free, off the grid and on food stamps, but we still needed money. There was no way around it. I hadn't worked legally since my high school paper route, and I figured that I should give respectable employment another try. In April, I left her to tend the cabin while I hitchhiked across the state to plant trees. Did I have to travel two hundred miles for a job? Maybe not, but when I got the opportunity to be a tree planter—a job I didn't even know existed—I was hooked. I had a vision of returning in triumph, thousands of dollars in my pocket and a forest to my name.

After hitching to Spokane, I spent the night at a commune where I'd crashed for long periods during the previous two years. Once again, they welcomed me, fed me, and gave me a bed. I slept for a few hours, then got up at 3 AM to stand on the sidewalk in the darkness and wait for a ride to the job site, far away in the woods. Already the thought crossed my mind that this was a crazy venture; who goes to work in the middle of the night? Soon a well-dented pickup truck pulled over. I tossed my pack into the bed and opened the door in time to catch the driver sweeping the litter from the passenger seat onto the floorboard. "I'm Peter," he said, sticking out a hand. Peter's vice-grip went along with shoulder-length red hair and brawny stature, a real Viking type. "It's a long way to the show," Peter said, and handed me a joint. "Gus is waiting for us." Peter laughed, like he'd said something funny, which I didn't understand, but I chuckled as if I did.

I knew Gus from the commune. Some old high school friends lived there and they'd invited me to take refuge after I'd survived several years of drugs, crime, homelessness, and high-risk activities. Surrounded by good people and food, it was a chance to start over. Instead, I used the downtime to throw myself into deep study of the game of chess, an obsession since my early teens. I poured over my copy of *Modern Chess Openings* as if it was scripture. Gus considered himself unbeatable at the game, and as soon as he realized I had some skill, he proposed a tournament between the two of us with no prize, just bragging rights as champion of the commune. The match lasted twenty games and took a month. Other people in the commune would idly watch when we played, but nobody else really cared about our struggle for supremacy. As it turned out, I won the bragging rights. This amounted to nothing since there was no one to listen to the bragging, but at least I didn't lose.

The chess match had happened in 1973, and after that I moved back to Seattle, met Deb, and convinced her to quit her job and flee to an impoverished life in the woods. We fished, hiked, and loafed through the winter until I received an invitation in the mail from Gus to join him planting trees in Northeast Washington. He had his own company with the curious name of The Swinging Hoedads. That sounded cool, so I wrote back with wild enthusiasm. I conjured a fantasy of what it would be like to wander through the woods, an elf with long-haired brethren, gracefully depositing trees in meadows and along gurgling brooks. Every so often, I imagined, when the spirit called, we'd take a break to inhale magic vapors and nibble at restorative hunks of waybread fresh from the ovens of Rivendell. Gus didn't try to talk me out of this delusion; in fact, I specifically remember his scrawled response and its paean to "outrageous dope." He also recommended the seasonal nature of the work, two to three months in the spring, then "you kick back on unemployment for the rest of the year." The schedule appealed to me.

Gus had been living on the job rather than the commune to eliminate the two-hour commute from the city. I had plenty of camping experience, so it seemed like a fine idea. As I sat in the passenger seat of Peter's truck, we bounced over miles of gravel roads cut through dense forest. These narrow green corridors looked identical in the pre-dawn gloom. Peter swerved wildly around ruts and banged straight over washboard corrugations; my insides were scrambled long before we arrived at the destination. When he finally stopped the truck, I stared through the windshield at the base of a steep slope. Even in the gloom I could see that forty acres of forest had been removed from the hillside, not a tree left standing. Peter said they'd logged it ten years ago and now so much time had passed—he waved his hand to encompass the whole site—it had regenerated a jungle of brush. He said this with an interesting combination of sadness and scorn. I studied my first clear-cut in the rising light. Here and there in the eight-foot-tall brush one could see the enormous, charred stumps of the former trees.

Parked on the road at the bottom of this slope was a 50s Buick sedan, cream yellow paint barely visible through layers of splattered mud. Peter tooted his horn; a grubby character soon rolled out from under the car. It was Gus. Peter said that he slept under the car because he didn't want to waste time setting up a shelter. "A distraction from work," Peter quoted, and laughed the same way as before. Now I understood it, the absurdity. As Gus walked over, I studied his appearance: bushy beard crusted with twigs, torn, mismatched clothes, the sheen of dirt on his skin, and a dazed, vacant smile. He looked like a disaster victim. At that point I realized I was going to need some very outrageous dope, indeed.

Gus flashed me a goofy grin and I got out of the truck to shake hands. Before we could start a conversation, a battered crew cab truck pulled in behind Peter's rig, blue smoke puffing from the exhaust. Four guys jumped out and sauntered over, a couple of them carrying shin-high work boots with spikes on the soles. Gus introduced me and we all shook hands, each trying to crush the other's fingers. The new guys also wore tattered clothing and looked like they lived in burrows. While the rest of us tested each other with banter, Peter started a campfire in a circle of rocks along the side of the road. Balancing a cast iron skillet across the circle, he threw in a cube of butter and a giant package of hamburger. "Breakfast," he said, chopping and stirring the meat with a spatula until it was less pink. We huddled around the pan and ate the greasy meat with spoons. After that, we chain-smoked pot until somebody broke the spell by saying they were getting to work.

Gus wasn't interested in teaching me how to do the job, so he handed off the task to an experienced planter, Lester, nicknamed "the Mo-lester." People often just called him "Mo." I didn't want to ask about the nickname, but I didn't have to, the dirty snickers were enough. At first, I was wary, but he turned out to be no stranger than anyone else on the crew and a lot less strange than some.

Lester gave me a bag to strap around my waist and a planting tool called a hoedad. The bag was about the size of a jumbo grocery sack, made from thick neoprene. The heavy hoedad balanced well in my hand as I hefted it. Lester showed me where the seedlings were cached, in giant cardboard boxes piled under a tarp. He pointed at the devastated slope and summarized the biopolitics. The job site, I learned, was called a "unit," a designation assigned by managers to surveyed sections of the National Forest. There were many units, and I came to understand that most of the endless forest had been divvied up into segments whose fate was ordained according to a resource utilization plan. The basic principle was simple: if a unit grew merchantable timber, then at some point it would be logged.

Lester lit a joint and we passed it back and forth while he provided more context for the job. When the master plan decreed, the timber went up for sale to the highest private bidder. The winning contractor then moved his equipment and crew to the unit and leveled it: everything standing was brought to the ground. This process was called "the show." Fallers cut down the trees with chainsaws, buckers de-limbed and sliced the trees to manageable lengths, then the logs were yarded out via heavy cable and enormous machines to a gravel landing where they could be loaded on trucks and hauled to the mill. Logging complete, the contractor packed up the gear and moved on to the next show. The remains of the unit resembled a carnage. Jumbled with woody debris known as slash, earth ripped open by the tracks and trails of heavy machines, the aftermath looked like hell. Later, the burn crews arrived to torch the debris, incinerating it to ash, preparing the ground for a new crop.

According to Lester, planting usually happened within a year of the burn and before the vegetation grew back. The unit we were on had been planted on that schedule, but most of the trees didn't survive. So, it was planted again, but most of those trees didn't survive, either. Why? Lester lit another joint and confessed that he wasn't sure, there could be a lot of reasons. Regardless, here we were, planting it yet again, a decade after the original clear cut. Meanwhile, the second growth and brush had taken over.

Gus, loaded with trees and ready for work, stopped for a puff of the joint, then handed it to me. As I inhaled, he said that I was supposed to plant a thousand trees a day. Lester cackled, while

Gus reclaimed the joint and walked off into the unit, smoke trailing from his fingers.

I followed Lester to some open ground where he showed me how to plant a tree. He made me plant one, too. He watched me without offering advice. "You're a natural," he said. "Just follow my line and plant one every twelve feet on a parallel line, twelve feet over. That's the grid for this unit: twelve by twelve. Yell if you need help." I quickly lost sight of him in the foliage.

I forced my way straight up the hill, pushing through branches of ironwood, searching for Lester's line of trees, which was not obvious to me. Whether it was the weed or general confusion, I ruminated with bovine dedication. Finally, I focused on a mantra: "What the fuck am I doing here? What the fuck am I doing here?" The bag of sopping wet tree seedlings strapped to my left hip felt like a sack of bricks and I kept cinching the waist belt to prevent it from sliding down my leg. In my right hand I carried the hoedad. The tool that gave the crew its name was a 4-inch wide by 16-inch-long steel blade bolted flat on the top of a 3-foot axe handle. I'd never seen its like. The blade is durable and heavy for superior ground penetration. Six to ten pounds heavy. This formidable tool can be swung over the head and driven into the earth, ideally sinking the blade to its full length. If you pull up on the butt of the handle, it pries the dirt under the ground, breaking apart the soil. Sliding a hand to the head of the hoe, you pull back the dirt. This reveals a narrow, rectangular hole, maybe a foot deep. A seedling is removed from the bag and the roots are dangled into the hole until they are straight. At that point the planter tamps the soil back in place with the blade, packing it firmly around the roots. A final stomp on the surface with the heel of your boot and you have just planted a tree.

The first few trees made me feel like a Boy Scout, and I dawdled over them, trying to make them perfect. By the time I'd planted a hundred, I hated the job. It crossed my mind that Gus had figured out a way to exact revenge for his chess defeat back in the commune. I had never worked so hard. The energy required to pound the earth into submission to plant tree after tree was like nothing I'd ever experienced, not in mountain climbing, wrangling firewood, planting gardens, playing sports, or any of the other labor-intensive activities I'd done. A new category was created against which all other things would be measured: tree planting. It wasn't just the effort of planting each one, it was the repetition, the ground-pounding, tree-hauling slog up and down steep slopes covered with every obstacle known to the woods. You had to be a madman.

We worked until dark, at which point, sitting around the fire waiting for the next pan of hamburger, I confessed that I had only managed to plant two hundred trees. Everyone laughed. Gus looked at me as if evaluating his mistake in putting me on the crew. I would have been ashamed, except that I was too exhausted to care. Besides, I had to focus on picking off the wood ticks. As I'd dragged my sweaty, stinking body through their leaf maze, I'd acquired more than a few. We all had them. Every day on this unit I gleaned ticks, up to twelve a day. Like monkeys, right after work, we rooted around in each other's hair. If they were embedded on open skin, we held a lit match to their rumps, causing them to back out, a nerve-wracking procedure for the host. We then scraped them up and placed the freed ticks on a hard surface where we used more matches and incinerated them. When they had dug into the scalp, it was too risky to use flame, so we tried to unscrew them, or, in desperation, just tore them off. Most that we found were loose on the body, wandering in a slow-motion quest for the perfect campsite. Without reflection, we terminated their stupid lives.

The ticks were creepy, but it hardly mattered. Never in my life had I been so tired. Workdays started at dawn and lasted till dusk. In between I beat the ground with my hoedad. Since we lived on the unit and there was no place to go, we worked. When we weren't doing that, we tortured ticks, smoked dope, and slept like rocks. At least I had my own tent where I could crawl in, close my eyes, and pretend that I was somewhere else.

2

The Means of Production

I abandoned myself to the routine. Gus had a contract with the Forest Service that would last all spring, and I accepted my role. Between the first and last light of each day, there were about fifteen hours of potential work. Gus attempted to maximize crew production by waking early and stumbling around the camp, banging things, and cursing at everyone to get up. I'd crawl out of my tent in the same clothes I'd worn the day before and join the others at the campfire. We'd eat whatever crap was available, usually not worth lingering over, gather our gear, and start working. Over the previous several years, I'd done enough mountaineering to be familiar with the challenges of camping in the rough, but nothing in my experience prepared me for the primitive character of the Swinging Hoedads work camp. We were grubs wallowing in the earth, eating peanut butter and hamburger, chain smoking dope, and sleeping like dead rocks. In Gus' mind, comforts like hygiene, food, and shelter were superficial. The important thing was getting trees in the ground and finishing the contract. He made one exception to the imperative of work: getting high.

As a result, an average of two to three hours daily would be spent smoking marijuana. It was a handy escape from the job.

Gus never lectured us, but I sensed his anxiety about completing the work on time. Given that he'd recruited a novice like me, he must have been desperate. He needed bodies. At the time, he was also fighting in court for his freedom. He'd signed up with the Marine Corps, then decided he didn't want to kill people. Our nation was up to its ass in Vietnam; I understood his reluctance, having wasted four years of my life avoiding that conflict. Gus took a more honorable approach, declaring his conscientious objections and refusing to participate in the war effort. Of course, the Marines didn't give a damn about his conscience and denied him status as a legitimate objector. As a result, he'd been entangled in court for years. I had no idea how much money his high-profile lawyer cost, but it was hard to imagine that tree planting would pay the bills. At least he wasn't in jail while the case dragged through the system. He didn't like to talk about it, probably because it sounded too much like complaining, a behavior he found distasteful. Gus carried the responsibilities of the job, but he didn't push them on anyone else. In fact, he rarely acted like a boss. At heart, he was an anarchist without a system; he just didn't like rules and regulations.

After getting past the first week and the shock of spending each day at hard labor, my muscles adapted to the extremes. I desperately wanted to keep up with the rest of the crew and I threw myself into it. Gradually, my skills improved. Peter, the big redhead, pounded trees in like a beast. He didn't brag about it; he seemed more interested in laughing at everything, a trait I admired but could never emulate. Gus was soft-spoken and stubborn, a mule who refused to admit shortcomings, let alone defeat. His endurance on the job gave me a good measure of how far I had to go. Lester, short and wiry, grew up in the labor trades, repairing masonry joints with his father on the towering brick chimneys of Chicago. He knew how to bend to the job. One of Gus' brothers was also on the crew, the first of many family recruits. He wasn't as hard-nosed as Gus, but he could do the work and do it well. His real name was Frank, but everyone called him Chang because he could screw up his face to look Asian. I'd seen the face, but it was a stretch. Everyone laughed, though. Like so many nicknames, it was demeaning on some level. If I was going to fit in with the macho boys, as well as learning how to work hard, I'd have to embrace the discourse. Swear words, I decided, were a good cover.

The rest of the crew consisted of short timers who worked for a few weeks and realized they'd rather be somewhere else, somewhere less brutal. Those who embraced the masochism, those were the men. I'd never been sure whether I belonged in that category, but I understood it to be the assigned goal. Strong, virile, competent: there were your young man's ambitions. Most of the time I was too anxious to command those qualities. Even though I'd been a rock climber and mountaineer, a decent chess player, a published writer, and a veteran of over a hundred acid trips, plenty of self-doubt remained. I needed something else to feel sure of myself. In the industrial forest, I was surrounded by a macho mindset, and I inhaled it right along with the dope. I became obsessed with getting faster, at first to keep up, then to beat everyone else. Beyond an aspiration, it became a necessity.

To increase my speed in planting, I learned to cut corners. It started at the landing with bagging up the trees. Delivered to the unit by the Forest Service in boxes, it was our job to keep the seedlings cool and moist. If there was shade, we'd put them in shade. Then we draped a tarp over the boxes and called it good. Next to the pile, Gus provided a bucket of water mixed with vermiculite. You took a tied bundle of fifty trees from the box, dipped the roots in the slurry, and racked the bundle in your bag, one after another, until the bag was full. That meant two to four hundred trees, depending on the size of the stock. Sometimes Forest Service representatives would stand around and watch us, in which case we'd treat the seedlings like they were our own children. When the rep wasn't around, or was sitting in his truck taking a nap, or happened to be walking the unit inspecting the planted sections, then we took liberties.

Seedlings look dainty taken one at a time, but quantities are heavy and bulky. Once a planter is out on the unit, it takes time and energy to return to the landing and get more trees—you can end up half a mile away. For efficiency, we stuffed as many seedlings in our bags as possible. Trees waterlogged with vermiculite are leaden, so we avoided the bucket if left to our own devices, or at the very least, shook off the vermiculite after dipping them. If the roots dried out before you could get them planted, well, you might have to do a mass grave in the woods to conceal the evidence. Or you could just plant them, what the hell. They'd look alive long enough to pass inspection. When the inspectors dug up selected trees, they wanted to see straight roots, that was essential. If the roots had been trimmed short at the nursery as planned, this was easy, but often they were trimmed poorly or not at all. The resulting progeny with their long, dangly roots would take forever to put in the ground, robbing us of precious seconds. We resolved the dilemma by taking a sharp axe, laying a handful of seedlings on a block of wood, and chopping them down to size. Fully loaded with modified stock, we'd slog off into the devastation of the clear cut, tilted to one side to offset the weight of the bag.

Within a couple of weeks, I realized that a thousand a day might be possible. After we finished the brush-choked tick hell, we moved on to a series of well-burned forty-to-sixty-acre clear cuts. These swaths of annihilated forest resembled Tolkien's descriptions of Mordor. Barren of life, covered with ash, it was true wasteland. But the open ground of the burned units, free of slash and brush, allowed me to focus on the mechanics of movement. Sustaining momentum, that was the trick. Drifting along in a haze of dope, I drove my body like an automaton. In time, I developed arms like steel cables, and did most of the hoedad work one-handed. I'd carry five or six trees in my left hand, flipping them into the holes opened by the arcing hoedad on the right. I was a steel-driving man, barely distinguishable from a machine. And it now seemed clear that becoming a machine was the key to becoming a man.

In time, I did become the fastest planter on the crew, but it took me two years. Not that I was any bigger or stronger than the others. My advantage lay in a maniacal analysis of movement, something I had learned from rock climbing, where the slightest details of kinetic efficiency made the difference between continuing up the pitch or falling off it. I trimmed away every wasted twitch of muscle. Never take three steps if you only needed two;

don't shuffle your feet; drive the hoe with power; don't waste time fumbling with trees; it's not the muscle, it's the rhythm. I pushed myself as hard as I could. I obsessed over stats like an athlete, timing myself and counting trees. And once I arrived at the pinnacle, I had no intention of losing my place.

The whole crew was fast, and we churned through units, moving from one to another, often setting up a camp at dusk so we could start work at dawn. One morning, after I'd become Gus' top money-maker, I woke to the *thunk thunk* of someone planting trees next to my tent. I muttered something rude and heard Gus' voice, taunting: "It's a two-thousand day." I knew that Gus lusted after this grail, but I'd be damned if I was going to let him get there first—and he had a head start. I threw on my clothes and bagged up—breakfast could wait. But breakfast never happened. The two of us planted for over twelve hours, pausing only to get more trees, shove down a peanut butter sandwich, and take hasty smoke breaks. We often planted side by side that day, trying to measure each other. It wasn't the slightest bit of fun; we'd become humorless fools. As it turned out, neither of us made two thousand. We planted until it was too dark to see the ground in front of us and had to quit. I did pass nineteen hundred and managed to plant a couple dozen more than Gus, which seemed to matter at the time, though I was too tired to celebrate. It was like another chapter of our chess match back in the commune.

Before they helped Gus start Swinging Hoedads, Lester and Peter had worked for several years with a notorious production contractor. That's where they'd all met and where Gus got the idea that he could run his own crew. They entertained us with stories of that outfit, most of which seemed like throwback tales to nineteenth century worker exploitation. In their old job, you'd fuck over your fellow crew member if it could advance you on the line, get you in the boss's good graces, and make a sliver more money. They hated it. Lester blamed dead trees on production quotas that encouraged quantity over quality. He'd slip into hyperbolic rants, raving about the absurdity of planting the same ground two or three or even five or six times. I listened to their critiques and developed my own hierarchy of blame, opting for a bigger scapegoat: "the system." Jamming trees in the dirt and bragging about how many you planted seemed idiotic. Yet that's exactly what I'd been doing. I'd read Marx; how could I not recognize in my own shadow the outline of the capitalist tool? Nobody wanted to be a tool for The Man; for one thing, it wasn't macho.

During frequent smoke breaks on the unit, Lester and I shared our stories, usually sitting on a log and passing the joint, doing our best to ignore the weather. We understood each other without explanation. I liked him because he loved poetry, silliness, and sarcasm—a man with my own priorities. I couldn't get enough of his bladed wit. When he turned it toward the politics and practice of tree planting, he showed no mercy. And none was deserved. We'd puff away and stare at the wreckage of the forest around us. Most citizens didn't see the results of timber industry greed. I never got used to it, what they called the harvest. I understood the need for wood products, I even wiped my ass with them, but the industrial forest was a hellscape. It didn't take long to understand that tree-planting was an essential component of that industry, the crowning rationale of the tree harvest. "A renewable resource," said the Forest Service. But was it?

The job required you to plant the acres and achieve a target density. For example, at twelve feet by twelve feet grid spacing, perfect density works out to about three hundred trees to the acre. However, units existed on actual ground, not in the two dimensions of management maps. Logging reduced these sections of forest to a jumble of debris. Burning the unit after the show was supposed to clear the debris. Sometimes it did, leaving a foot of ash that had to be scalped off before finding the mineral soil for planting. Other units burned poorly and remained submerged under a daunting cover of slash; sometimes you couldn't even see dirt for the leftover logs and branches. These units presented problems in three dimensions, forcing you to crawl over crisscrossed logs and into open pockets where a tree or two could be planted before climbing through the next puzzle of logs to find another pocket. Every unit was different and presented its own challenges. Besides slash, the reality of planting forced you to deal with a host of other obstacles: old rotten logs, gullies with creeks, solid ledge just under the surface, thickets of brush, boulders and outcrops, bone-jarring hidden rocks, giant stumps, landslides, and steep terrain that could not be planted by any means, let alone by a stoned hippie pounding away with a hand tool.

The Forest Service didn't expect to see a tree every twelve feet. After all, they knew the ground; they had to crawl through the same units for their inspections. In sample plots, they'd count the trees and dig up a few to assess the character of the work. They didn't like to engage with the horror show sections of the unit; if your tree count was sparse in the hard parts but tight in the easy ones, and your roots were generally straight, they'd often give you a pass.

Sitting in the wasteland, getting wasted on weed, one day Lester and I found enlightenment. We needed to stop counting trees like it meant anything and start thinking in acres.

"It's not about how many trees YOU plant," he said during our first joint break, "it's how fast the crew covers the total ground... as long as we still pass inspection."

I said, "It's not about how many trees, it's about how few!"

He giggled, coughing smoke like a dying engine. "As long as it passes inspection."

I agreed with him. The trees were important, but not as much as the inspectors. This lesson about the working world stayed with me for decades: it's not so much about doing the job, it's about appearing to do the job.

3

Crummy Life

During my first season with the Swinging Hoedads, we carped at Gus about camping on each unit. We'd have to move every day or two from one fucked-up spot to another like hyperactive migrants. There was barely time to pitch a tent; no wonder Gus slept under his car. These places were all the same; we set up on the gravel landing where the loggers had staged the business end of the show. Most landings featured depressing arrays of debris: bulldozed piles of rock and gravel, left over fuel barrels, broken cables, oil spills, and whatever trash logs and scrap wood weren't worth hauling out. Basically, we lived in the garbage dumps of industrial forestry, like homeless people in abandoned factories. Every time we drove past an inviting glade in the woods on our way to the next unit, we'd extoll its virtues: "Wouldn't *that* make a nice place to camp? And look, there's a stream for water!" Like children begging for a treat, we finally wore him down.

I pointed at a Forest Service map and identified a central place where we could make one camp to last till the end of the contract. I argued for improved efficiency because we wouldn't have to waste time taking stuff down and packing whenever we finished a unit. True, we'd have to drive back and forth from the central camp, but it wasn't all that far, and we promised Gus that he would see an increase in production since we'd be so much happier. I don't think he believed our nonsense, but he got tired of hearing it, and caved in. He got back at us by bringing it up whenever he wanted to blame something for going wrong.

Not that we ever got to relax and appreciate these idyllic campsites. We drove to the unit at dawn and returned at dusk. Otherwise, it was too dark to see anything. At least we didn't have to break camp every couple of days and sleep on the wasteland. Gus resisted quality-of-life improvements but came to accept that his minimalism did not play well with the crew, no matter how good the dope. He started to upgrade his operation. He even got his own tent. Before that, though, he ditched the Buick and purchased a utility vehicle, in this case, an International Travelall, a classic four-wheel drive workhorse. It came in orange, visible for miles, and could hold six workers and lots of gear. In the lexicon of the woods, a personnel carrier, no matter what kind, was called "the crummy." With good reason, for no matter how clean and neat it may have started its career as a work vehicle, the result was a dented and careless squalor.

After we started driving to the unit from a central camp, the crummy provided our only option for shelter during the workday. We always carried rain gear, because it rained often, but it was hard to smoke a joint in a downpour. When the weather was at its worst, we hid out in the crummy, reluctant to crawl into our clammy gear and get back to work. It didn't take long before

Gus' new rig reeked of wet socks, sweat, orange peels, and marijuana.

We ate our meals in the crummy, or if the weather was fair, we sat in the gravel and leaned back against the tires. I say meals but I mean peanut butter and jelly sandwiches. Gus had a curious indifference to food, even though he'd consume great quantities when it was in front of him. If you asked any questions about the next meal, like when or what, he shrugged, reached under the driver's seat, and withdrew a Hershey's chocolate bar. He bought these by the carton and kept them out of sight. The crew were not allowed the chocolate bars, they were Gus's private reserve. What the crew did have were oranges, peanut butter, and dope. Crew consumables were purchased in bulk and owned as common property. A crate of oranges could always be found in the back alongside the planting gear. Jars of peanut butter and jam rolled around on the floor. Bread loaves ended up sequestered here and there, often squashed. And the dope sat in a large metal pan that Gus used in the off-season for sifting gold out of Montana streams. We'd dump an ounce or two of leaf into the pan, throw in a pack of rolling papers, and park it on the front or back seat for convenience.

The crummy was a sanctuary. Within those confines we ate, smoked, and talked. We spent so much time there that if it'd been a chapel, we'd be holy. This is how it worked: say you've been planting for hours, and your bag of trees is getting low, it's been raining the whole time, or it's threatening rain, or there might be a lightning storm, or the sun is out and it's boiling hot, or you've developed a hole in your glove and you need a new pair, or whatever—the excuses are endless. But you've determined in your own mind that it's essential to get back to the crummy. And while you're back there you might as well smoke a doobie. Your crewmate agrees, of course. You smoke one. You discuss the reasons why it's not yet time to get back to work, and while you do that, you smoke another one. By the time you finish the second joint, a new crew member shows up and of course you might as well smoke one with him. Eventually it becomes a kind of game as to how long you can avoid the job and stay in the crummy. We got very good at this game. Gus didn't help—he was as bad as any of us when it came to the dope distraction. It's not hard to understand; the work was brutal and intense, and I never heard anyone claim to enjoy it. So, for the sake of avoidance, we'd sit in the crummy, pass the gold pan back and forth, and smoke our brains out.

Gus fronted the money for food and dope and took it out of our earnings at the end of the season. You could get an early draw if you needed cash, but there was only one payday: the day after the last tree was planted. Like credit from the company store, you had a shock when it was time to settle and discovered how much money you'd spent on drugs and oranges. But the weed seemed essential, so we indulged. We tore through it so fast that we had to buy in bulk. In those days a pound of high-grade marijuana could cost anywhere from $1200 to $1800, depending on source and quality. Lester knew people who could provide those quantities. When the stash got low, we'd make dope runs. These were popular since they involved leaving the unit for a day or two and going into the city where you might be able to take a shower.

One time, as Lester and I sat in the crummy and smoked through the dwindling remains in the gold pan, we agreed that we needed to get more. Running out was unthinkable. I volunteered to approach Gus about the cash. I knew he'd gone down the hill below the landing to plant by himself. I couldn't see him, but I heard the thunking of his hoedad, so I jumped over the edge of the road and scrambled down through the slash to find him. When I approached, I saw that he wore the same outfit he'd been wearing for the last month, torn pants, and a shredded flannel shirt. We all wore a version of that outfit because no matter what you brought to the job, it ended up battered to threads. I hallooed and said that Lester and I were going to make a run for dope, and did he have enough money for that?

"How much do you want?" He asked.

"Eighteen hundred ought to do it."

I expected that we would arrange to retrieve the money from camp after work, but he reached into his pocket, pulled out a fat roll of cash and with exaggerated drama peeled off two thousand dollars in hundreds. He handed it to me with a sly grin. He must have had at least five grand. I was amazed—it's not like there was anything to buy on the unit. Maybe just Gus's way of being prepared. I asked why the fuck he carried all that cash, but he didn't say. Perhaps he felt more secure, knowing it was in his pocket. My guess is that he'd been waiting for this moment, and it was just another way to blow our minds, a favorite preoccupation of his.

We smoked a lot—an excess, no doubt. With alcohol, you can easily get too loaded to plant trees, but not marijuana. Lord knows we tried. Our excuse was that it helped cope with the conditions, and even though it's a lame excuse, there is some truth in it. Often, you'd spend the whole day encased in neoprene rain gear, hood up and head down, bathing in your own sweat. Neoprene is perfectly waterproof, no moisture can get in or out, leaving the planter in a permanent state of self-generated dampness, a marginal improvement over being soaked in the steady rain. These conditions were easier to tolerate if you were stoned. Days huddled in rain gear, under the cowl, lost in the rhythm of work, you could surrender to the cascading stream of consciousness and chug along in oblivion.

Time often disappeared within the toil. Once, it had been raining hard for several days when the thought crossed my mind that the air was heavy. Indeed, the humidity was high, but the air itself felt thick, like syrup, forcing me to move slower and work harder. The pace of the world reduced to a crawl. I obsessed over this until I had to share my observation with the rest of the crew: "Have you noticed the heavy air?" Oh yes, they had. We were all moving slowly, no doubt about it. Never mind the dope, dammit: heavy air was slowing us down. In the following days, this became a refrain: "Heavy air today, don't you think?" All it took was a mention of the phrase and suddenly the work was harder, movement slower, and a dense fuzz settled in the brain. Heavy air was a serious drag. The only antidote was to get back to the sanctuary of the crummy as soon as possible and smoke another joint.

4

Flotation Devices

I floated through the days in a trance, unable to distinguish one from another except by the occasional novelty. It didn't take much to qualify as a novelty. I remember the day that I returned to the crummy for lunch and found Lester and Peter in the front seat, consulting a copy of Penthouse magazine. I sat behind them and looked over their shoulders. They passed it back and forth, thumbing through pages like it was a dictionary and they needed the right word. First one of them would hold up an image and solicit the other's opinion. Judgments were succinct, on the order of "yeah, man" and "oh yeah." Then the other would find a counterexample, as if it were a competition. I looked at the pictures and kept silent. I never understood how to fit in with this sort of male bonding. It was supposed to be a fun thing that guys did, but it stirred up unresolved questions for me, a turbulence that left me paralyzed. I knew the portraits were provocations from an absurd sexual mythology, but I looked at them anyway. So, there we were, a grubby huddle of men in a machine parked way out in the woods, dreaming about flesh we'd never touch. Like everything else, in time these periodicals migrated to the floor of the crummy, where they met a tattered and soggy fate.

My contributions to crew culture were less exotic, but no less absurd. For example, I got Lester hooked on singing "Frosty the Snowman." It just popped into my head one day as I churned back and forth across the unit planting as fast as I could—suddenly, there it was. Of course, I was stoned out of my mind. It hit like the neutron bomb of earworms. I planted faster to get away from it. Not a chance. When our lines met, I looked at Lester and sang to him as loudly as I could. "Frosty the Snowman, da da da da da...." A look of panic appeared in his eyes, but of course he started singing it, too. There was no release. After a couple of hours, we were still singing and humming it, so we stopped and smoked more dope, embracing the problem as a solution. The ditty faded after a week or so, although it kept popping up for years; we never escaped its echo.

Lester responded with improvised operas. As this required some creativity, it captured my interest. We collaborated on scenarios, protagonists, villains, and choruses that kept us amused for hours. When our planting lines came together, we'd share our latest inspirations. I cracked up every time he sang in a booming bass: "Ho ho ho, here comes the inspec-tor!" It was all quite hilarious, though I doubt any of this material could stand up to the light of day.

Despite the heavy pot use and our demented mentalities, we applied ourselves to the craft of planting trees. We wanted to figure out how to cover the most ground with the least amount of effort. This required innovation. Traditional crews used a single strategy: put twenty or more planters in the field at a time, following one behind the other on parallel lines, the fastest guys in front. They would pound straight up or down slopes, attempting to maintain formation the whole way. It works if everyone plants at a predictable speed. The crew chugs along in sync, each planter holding a consistent spacing with the others. When you run into complications on your line (slash or brush, for example), you must plant faster to stay ahead of the guy behind. This person may or may not be facing similar obstacles, but you can't slow down because that creates a ripple effect. If the planter behind you gets impatient with your progress and tries to pass, taking over your line, you will be tempted to bark at him because losing your place in line is a form of losing status on the crew. If he doesn't retreat, and you're really pissed, you can run over and punch him in the face. This was part of the tradition. I never hit anyone on the job, although once I made it to lead planter, any attempt to pass me ignited my fury. Instead of throwing punches, I'd shift into hyperdrive and plant so fast that the upstart realized the error of his ways. Sometimes this stunt worked. If it didn't, I'd lay on an extra measure of glaring, swearing, and bad vibes. I'd always thought of myself as a peaceful fellow, but tree planting suggested other possibilities.

In the cutthroat crews, a foreman (sometimes the lead planter) yells at everybody to speed up, stay in line, and stop fighting. We didn't have such a foreman in the Swinging Hoedads, we had Gus and his genial temperament. He wasn't about to tell people what to do, let alone yell at them. He held his crew in thrall by keeping us isolated in the forest and dependent on him for food and dope. Then he let nature take its course.

With little to think about day after day except tree planting, we just wanted to plant the damn things and go home.

I don't know when we hit upon the idea of working laterally along terrace lines as a planting formation, or who thought of it first, but it became our creed. We fit the principles to the topography of clearcuts in the National Forests of the Northwest. In the 1800s, the federal government gave away most of the fertile lowland forest to private companies as incentives to build railroads. Capitalists didn't want the more challenging terrain of the mountains, and eventually that became the grounds of the National Forest. Good timber grew in the hills; you just had to log it off the slopes. To get to those slopes, you had to build roads, so the Forest Service built almost four hundred thousand miles of them. In the NW, an access road to a unit sliced laterally along a slope to form the upper or lower boundary of a clearcut. As part of the roadbuilding, an area was dozed flat to carve a landing big enough for the logging gear. After the logging show finished and moved on, reforestation began at the same landing, ground zero for the unit.

During the drive to a new unit, we always wondered what lay ahead. To avoid disappointment, we assumed the worst—another nightmare filled with slash, brush, and rock. Either that or a charred landscape of suffocating ash. Excited with dread, we'd roll joint after joint as we bounced over the crappy roads. Finally, Gus would bring the crummy to a halt, we'd crawl out of the smoke chamber and stumble to the edge of the landing. We'd line up, side by side, and piss into the fresh hell as we studied the terrain. By the time we'd drained our bladders, we'd have devised the opening scheme for our planting maneuvers.

Water runoff carves gullies down every sloped unit. These gullies delineate the terrain into vertical sections. Instead of marching up and down the slope *en masse* and ignoring natural features, with our new method we assigned one planter to each vertical section. When the landing was at the top of the unit, two guys planted a line straight down on each side of a gully all the way to the bottom boundary. From there they turned and went in opposite directions, following an imagined horizontal terrace line until encountering another gully or significant natural feature. Then they'd bump up twelve feet to the next "terrace" and work back above the line just planted. The two planters would meet up at the original gully, say hi or sing a bit of "Frosty the Snowman," then climb to the next terrace and head off along a new contour. By repeating this maneuver, planters could work back and forth on horizontal lines, slowly ascending the slope as they filled the area between gullies. We called this "floating."

There were enormous benefits to this method. For one thing, moving on the contour is much easier than going up and down. Also, a planter worked on top of his own line. Having just planted a terrace, he knew where the trees were. Following another planter's line often resembles a scavenger hunt for the tiny trees hidden amidst the brush, weeds, slash, and whatnot. A sure way to get pissed off at your buddy. While floating, you could develop micro strategies to deal with unplantable ground, putting more trees closer together around the margins of bad spots, ensuring the target density for the acreage. Thus, the planter worked the unit like a three-dimensional puzzle rather than a linear race. In addition, there were social benefits. You could stop for smoke breaks with the guy across the gully when you bumped, with no crew of speed freaks breathing down your neck. Some days it was even pleasant to sit and stare across the forest remains and chat. It also allowed a planter to work in proximity to crew members that he liked, avoiding the annoying ones—and there were always annoying ones.

One season Gus hired a teenager from LA who claimed to be the nephew or cousin of Alice Cooper. Maybe he was, we had no way of knowing, even when he told us that Alice's real name was Vince. The kid talked compulsively, mostly about life in Southern California, the center of the universe. He told a lot of stories about his uncle, pretty much the kind of thing you expected to hear about a rock star. On the unit, the kid always packed a .44 magnum pistol in a holster on his hip, opposite his tree bag. When I first saw him strap it on before work, I thought he was joking. At the very least, it's a heavy gun. I couldn't figure out why he wanted to drag such a thing around the clearcut, but he and the gun were inseparable. Maybe growing up in LA does that to you. Every now and then, he'd take it out and blow a few rounds into a stump. I always wanted to duck when I heard the cannon-like reports, but I settled for the next best thing: I stayed as far the fuck away from him as I could. After the thunderous ejaculations, he'd cackle like a hyena because it was too hilarious for words. Gus, of course, never set any limits with him. He worked with us for a season or two, then thankfully went back to LA where he could play Dirty Harry with his people.

After three years of working in Idaho and NE Washington, Gus won a contract on the Olympic Peninsula. We had six weeks to plant over a thousand acres, a daunting task for a small crew. At first, it seemed impossible. The units were scattered through the heart of the Quinault National Forest, the rainiest place in the continental United States. When it wasn't raining, the earth cloaked itself in mist and fog. The permeating damp creates an environment so lush that the total biomass exceeds any known tropical zone. In Quinault, units don't burn so much as smolder. On every clearcut the ground was steep and bristling with layers of unburned slash. I looked at the first unit, started swearing, and laced up my boots extra tight. We all wore them by now, the high-topped, spike-soled logging boots known as calks but always pronounced "corks." These proved essential for climbing through slash, saving time, and reducing the risk of falling off a log. As a bonus, they offered opportunities to show off by dancing along the bark like drunk squirrels.

We had perfected our floating terrace system, and we used it to our advantage on the Quinault terrain. Instead of burrowing straight through all the slash, we planted around most of it. Far from slowing us down, we covered the acres faster, because there was so much unplantable ground. On that contract I worked forty-five consecutive days—we all did—averaging eleven hours a day. Long, winding commutes from a base camp in the valley bracketed these sessions of labor. I was in top shape and never seemed to get tired. The longer it went on, the stronger I felt. We found pleasure in the kinetics of the work, and the tougher it was, the more pleasure we got out of doing it—and doing it together. Inspired by our competence, we threw ourselves at the job, finishing the last unit on the last day. When we converged at the crummy, Gus was grinning like he'd just won the lottery, which maybe he had. But we'd done it for ourselves, too, because we could.

| 34 | - FLOTATION DEVICES

5

Burnt Orange

Despite our manly pride in the work, we couldn't escape the underlying reality: reforestation remained an afterthought in a vast industrial process. Cynicism dogged us from the shadows, reminding us of uncomfortable truths. The industry was a capitalist scam, like every other resource extraction ploy, mining money from nature. A tactic that goes back thousands of years to Gilgamesh, the Sumerian clearcutter, the guy that leveled the cedars of Lebanon for glory and a fortune in timber. Despite the history of human onslaught against trees, we drew energy from the hope that one day there'd be another forest standing over our labor. As tree planters, we needed a new myth, a way to contain our knowledge of the dark economic politics without abandoning a basic devotion to trees. So, we did what we had to do, and we got stoned to do it. Marijuana was the anodyne of our conscience. Without something, the damage was too painful to witness, from clearcut to clearcut, all across the Northwest, the devastation of an ecosystem. We acted tough and unflappable, but that was an act, our concession to the necessary machismo.

Maybe we'd taken too much acid or spent too much time daydreaming about Tolkien's forests. Whatever the source of our affinities, trees mattered.

After the Forest Service ran enough inspections to assess our units, they stopped bitching about our unconventional planting formations. We hit their density targets better than traditional crews and our roots were mostly straight. I'm not sure they understood what we were doing and how we did it, but they didn't ignore the results.

No one tended or watered the trees after we planted them, making it a job best suited for the wet season. In NE Washington and Northern Idaho, where the Swinging Hoedads did most of their work, the wettest season was spring, but it wasn't reliable. Days could go by without a drop of rain. As summer approached, the temperature climbed, and the soil dried. The Forest Service encouraged us to select planting sites behind logs, rocks, or any natural shade to utilize the lingering ground moisture. If we could, we would, but that only accounted for a few trees. In a flash of inspiration, no doubt drug fueled, Lester started placing a handy rock or piece of wood to shade the seedling. With the fever of the evangelist, he urged us to follow suit. "It's piss easy," he said. He wasn't wrong. Units are covered with debris, all the stuff churned up during the wreckage of logging. A planter could grab a chunk of wood and plop it on the south side of the seedling in a matter of seconds. Maybe this made a difference in survival, so why not? And if there was nothing in the vicinity, well then, we moved on to the next spot and left the little tree to its destiny.

At first, the Forest Service inspectors were puzzled by our shades. I don't think they'd seen anyone do stuff like that. They offered sincere admiration, which egged us on to greater feats of improvisation. When I was really stoned, I'd find myself getting carried away, gathering several sticks to pile up shade fences, tarrying longer than necessary over a spot to build something clever or even amazing. During breaks, we'd praise the masterpieces we'd seen on each other's lines or brag about our own constructions.

We labored on through unit after unit while hope and discouragement flickered back and forth in unpredictable oscillations. The units with poor survival were always a downer. Some had been planted as many as five times over a decade and still only 20% of the ground was populated with living trees. We convinced ourselves this was an outcome of old school production planting, speed over quality. Of course, we weren't like those crews; we were different, we were stoner hippy tree freaks, and we wanted a legacy of more than acres of dead sticks. In the back of our brains and amidst the industrial routines, the elvish dreams flourished. We had to work harder for those fantasies, but then we were tougher and smarter than everybody else and looked for every excuse to prove it.

Our relationship with the Forest Service involved mutual, cautious tolerance, never far from the next tempest. We were hard on them, it's true. We called them the "Forest Circus," or just "the Circus," laying it on with a sneer. I knew they couldn't help representing their bureaucracy; it's not like they had a choice. For one thing, they were forced to wear those hideous algae-colored shirts and brown khakis, not exactly a uniform bound for glory. Even the loggers made fun of them, as if they were not quite real men. But then no contractor likes inspector-types; the antagonism is natural and involves money, the vortex of trouble.

You never knew when a conflict would appear. For example, there was the situation with orange peels in Idaho. Now oranges are good food, an excellent source of nutrients, little bright balls of vitality, which is why we liked them. The juice provided an exquisite sensation as it trickled past our weed-enhanced taste buds. A moment of bliss to please the fiery brain. Smoke a joint, eat an orange. Do it again. We'd sit in the crummy, avoiding work, smoking, and eating slices. Peels were tossed out the windows. We had all grown up with Lady Bird Johnson's admonishments to "beautify America" and we did not drive down the road, chucking beverage cans into the ditch like many Americans. But this was the landing of the logging show and under no stretch of anyone's lexicon did it qualify as "America the beautiful." Bulldozed gravel, debris, trash: the landing summarized the devastation. When loggers folded up the machines, they wanted their expensive gear on the next show as soon as possible. Detailing the unit was not a priority.

Then along came the Swinging Hoedads to occupy the landing, brazenly smoking dope and tossing orange peels like confetti. We never looked at the peels as a downgrade to the scenery. If we even thought of orange peels as a visual distraction, we'd shrug and say "well, they're organic." It wasn't something we dawdled over; we'd peel off the skins and throw them out the window.

One day a Forest Service inspector told us to knock it off, it was littering. "You're spoiling the view," he said. We stared at him, curious to regard a man who could say such a thing. A rebuttal seemed impossible. Beyond the landing lay the war zone of the clear-cut. A scene of pillage where a giant, monstrous god had consumed a whole section of forest in a frenzy of destruction. Complaining that a handful of peels didn't belong on the gravel was like complaining about a carpet stain at the entrance to Hell. From that point on, we made a big show of discarding peels on the landing, especially when the inspector was around, going out of our way to eat more oranges and generate more peels. You could even tell where we'd parked the previous day by the outline of discarded rinds. Orange crummy, orange peels, that was us, take it or leave it.

When I wasn't hating them, I felt sorry for the inspectors. Tree-planting supervision was not a plum assignment within the Forest Service. Many inspectors were young men starting on the government career ladder. I'm sure they were instructed not to get too chummy with the unpredictable tree planters, well known to get surly if their pay was docked. Most inspectors adopted a neutral demeanor, passing on their results directly to Gus without comment. But some were unpredictable themselves, or perhaps just bored with the hours spent in their trucks, driving the endless dirt roads at fifteen miles per hour and not a bit faster. Way out in the woods, many miles from headquarters, who was to say what they could or couldn't do? Some of these guys found us entertaining, like we were a newly discovered species, and they were content to lean on their trucks and chat away, watching us while we smoked joint after joint. We always made a point of offering them a puff, just to torment them. One inspector surprised us by accepting. He was an amiable fellow—we all liked him—and I'm sure he'd smoked before, though maybe not our high-grade stuff, and certainly not at work. He seemed a bit unsteady when he got back into his brand new government-leased pickup. Within a hundred yards of the landing, he drove over the edge of the road and bashed into a stump. We howled with delight and punched each other in the shoulders, then sauntered over to help push the truck back on the road. For days, we speculated on the excuses he would need to explain the dents. Subsequent offers to join us in communion were refused.

One year Gus secured a fall contract in Northern Idaho, a rare offering during the dry season. The Forest Service bragged about a new experiment in forest management, a large one-hundred-acre unit that had been full of larch and pine and other undesirable species. Someone had an idea: wouldn't it be neat if it was covered with Douglas Fir instead? So, they logged it over the summer, burned it in September, and told us to plant it in October. It turned out that most of the fallen trees didn't offer much value as merchantable timber, and they didn't bother to yard them out, just left them where they lay. With plenty of fuel, the unit burned hot and long, aided by the cloudless weather of late summer. It burned so well, in fact, that it was still on fire when we got there to replant it. Flames danced along charred logs while plumes of smoke rose from smoldering roots and stumps.

We didn't even blink at this absurdity; we gave the unit the once-over and bagged up the eager seedlings of Douglas Fir. Three steps onto the unit and I stopped in my tracks: a blanket of fresh, fluffy ash covered the ground a foot deep. Usually when we got to a burned unit the rains and snows of the intervening winter had compressed the ash down to an inch or two of crusty material. You scraped it away with the hoedad, sometimes with a single swipe. On this unit, as soon as blade met earth, feathery ash flew up in clouds and lingered in the air. According to the scientists who study these things, ash is toxic to the respiratory system and should be avoided. Hard to do when your job required you to stir up a fog of it, step into the middle, bend over to plant a tree, take three steps and roil up another cloud, one tree after another, all day long. Within a week we hacked black phlegm in the morning and coughed throughout the day.

Once you scraped the ash off a spot and got down to mineral soil, then you discovered an alarming truth about the mineral content. The thought entered your mind that maybe it wasn't soil at all, a notion reinforced every time your hoedad clanged as you tried to drive it into the ground. Never mind that you had squandered your lungs scraping ash to find the red soil, it turned out to be a veneer on solid bedrock and you couldn't plant there. We started to probe the ground before scalping, poking hoe blades through the ash trying to find enough space between rocks to cram a tree. After about the tenth time of feeling that unique pain resonating through my arms from slamming a hoedad full force into a buried rock, I stopped, straightened up and surveyed the unit. It didn't take a geologist to see that we were standing on a hundred acres of granite covered with shallow soil. Ledge protruded everywhere and the only species that had been growing were those that adapt well to thin soil, spreading their roots horizontally to embrace the rock. Such trees don't get tall or thick, but they can grow and make a forest. These idiots had just cut it all down and burned it.

After a few days of pounding away at this shit, the inspector started to panic because we weren't getting very many trees in the ground. We poked and probed, scalped here and there, tried to find spots. You could spend staggering amounts of energy wrestling with the effort to plant a tree, then, just for something different, you'd have to make a detour around a log or stump because it was on fire. Summoning a straight face, I asked the inspector how far away from flames he wanted us to plant the trees. "Oh, you know, a ways."

"Sure, a ways it is."

The crew verged toward rebellion. The unit was a disaster and seemed like it would last forever, a special hell for tree planters. Finally, Gus had enough and called the Forest Service to negotiate a contract adjustment. The Circus administration flew into a tizzy. This was, after all, their brilliant experiment in forestry, showing how they could turn unproductive ground into valuable real estate. The managers descended on the unit. Many arrived in a fleet of new trucks from the local ranger district. Two helicopters of Very Important People flew in from the National Forest headquarters in Coeur d'Alene. The unit buzzed with khaki-suited officials. They walked around on the roads and landing, peering at the unit, talking with Gus and with each other. None of them sullied their footwear by walking into the desolation of ash. This went on all day and then, in true government fashion, they left without a decision. In the end, nobody wanted to take responsibility for the bogus experiment. Whoever had drawn it up had failed to consider the geology and ecology of the site. Not the first or last time that happened. Left with no recourse other than defaulting the contract, we labored on to complete the unit, literally holding our breath. Months later the bureaucrats eked out a concession and paid a slightly higher rate per acre. The whole crew got a small bonus check in the mail. Just in time to celebrate the end of the constant cough.

6

Men, Mosquitoes, and Machines

Gus loved the crummy; it was his darling. You wouldn't say the crew loved it; we saw it as a refuge from work and the weather, a necessity rather than a romance. But to Gus, the machine represented more than sanctuary; it served as an extension of his being. And we did admire its robust practicality. Besides the lively orange color, it featured solid engineering, a bull-like four-wheel-drive, and an electric winch mounted on the front bumper. Never mind that the International Corporation didn't build any two vehicles with the same exact parts and didn't keep track of the differences from model to model. Getting replacement parts often required sustained inquiries over thousands of miles. When the rig worked, which was most of the time, the Travelall was a beast. Gus embraced this nature—embodied it himself, in fact.

The remote units of Northern Idaho forced us into long, pummeling drives on crappy roads. We numbed ourselves by passing the gold pan back and forth. One time, we'd been riding and smoking through the industrial forest for at least an hour. No one wore a watch, so it was hard to tell. Gus pointed out that if we'd camped on the unit, we wouldn't be doing this, a comment that drew jeers and laughter. We were totally blitzed by the time we got to the job. The road traversed the clear-cut and ended halfway across the broad, open slope. As we approached the landing, Gus asked if we were close enough to where we should start planting, a common question, since he deferred strategy decisions to the crew.

"Sure," we all agreed.

"No," he countered. "I think we can get closer." He shifted into low range on the four-wheel drive and drove the fucking thing right over the edge of road and down the embankment into the unit itself. "I think we can get much closer," he shouted, and steered the crummy over sticks, branches, and rocks, grinding and scraping across the slope, gunning the engine to keep momentum so we didn't slide down the hill. He dodged a stump or two, twisting the wheel like a bronco-riding cowboy. The rest of us braced ourselves as best we could. Despite Gus' commitment to forward progress, eventually the crummy couldn't maintain traction and slid sideways about twenty feet, jamming up against a big stump. "Hmmm," he said, "I don't know if we can get any closer than this."

We crawled out of the rig to assess the situation, pretending that everything was normal, another day in the woods with the Swinging Hoedads. I wondered what Gus was thinking. We weren't going to simply drive back to the landing hundreds of feet away and uphill. Not through the stumps and debris. The rest of us scrambled to a nearby log and sat on it like pigeons on a fence, waiting to see what would happen next. Gus was undaunted; he seemed downright cheerful. Now, he got to use his precious winch. The winch contained about a hundred feet of cable on a spool, ending in a big hook. Gus grabbed the hook and climbed the slope, unwinding the cable. He wrapped it around a big stump and hooked it in a loop. Returning to the crummy, he activated the winch, which only does one thing: it winds the cable back onto the spool. Since the cable was tied off to an immovable object, the only way the winch could retrieve its line was by dragging the crummy with it. Obediently, the machine crawled up the slope, crunching through sticks and branches. When it was far enough for Gus's purposes, he stopped the winch, climbed into the driver's seat, and cranked the front wheels to the left as hard as he could. Getting out, he released the brake on the winch cable. The rig slid backwards downhill, slewing around due to the cocked front wheels. We saw right away what he was up to; by changing the anchor points of the cable and repeating this maneuver, he could eventually turn the rig 180 degrees, until it was aimed at the landing. It only took five more operations of the dutiful winch to achieve this goal. A cable placement in line with the landing pulled the rig back through the battery of rocks and branches we'd crossed on the descent. With a final set, Gus was able to drag the two-ton machine back up onto the road. While he did all this, which took a couple of hours, the crew sat on the log with the gold pan, smoking and watching the show, offering humorous commentary. He grinned at everything we said but kept his own counsel. Too happy for words, he didn't seem to mind that not a tree got planted until after the performance. We had to work extra hard to make up for the delay, but nobody cared, it was such a good show that it became part of crew legend: "Remember when Gus drove off the landing?" Yes, we did.

One year Gus asked if I would stick around after the crew finished the season and help him with an add-on contract. It involved two small units in Idaho's Priest River district, just a few acres each, nearly flat ground and with a minimum of slash. He conjectured that the two of us could race through this project and make quick money. Flattered by the offer, I succumbed to his silver-tongued promises of easy work and extra cash. When the crew dispersed in mid-June, the days were long and hot, not the best weather for planting. Gus and I shrugged it off as nothing more than the latest adversity. Fit and confident, we anticipated the possibility of record-setting tree counts. Both of us, despite our desire to plant thriving forests, couldn't let go of the gunslinger mentality. Tree planting glory, no matter how illusory, feeds on the swagger of individual achievement. And that requires numbers, big numbers.

We drove Gus's '57 Willys pickup to Priest River and left the Travelall parked at his home in Bonners Ferry. The Willys, blood red, with a boxy, military-style body, was a charming, quaint contraption, a bit of a rattletrap but it could scamper around offroad like a mechanized goat. Now that was a machine that drew my affections and I lusted after one, but they were already off the market, eclipsed by sleeker designs. Not everyone's aesthetic, perhaps, but for me the Willys epitomized the apex of mechanical funk. Sitting in the passenger seat as we arrived at the job, arm out the window, I felt pretty damn good, stone cool, and ready for some gravy cruising.

Temperatures in Northern Idaho were expected to hit 100 degrees that day, and we wore T-shirts and light pants. We stuffed our bags and floated off into our chosen enclaves. As I bent over to plant my first tree, at least half-a-dozen mosquitoes drilled into my back, right through the thin T-shirt. I finished the tree smartly and raced off to the next spot. If I'd trotted away for a hundred yards, the mosquitoes would have milled around in confusion before settling back to await another transient mammal. But twelve feet to the next planting spot didn't take me out of their sensory zone. No, they buzzed along behind, and as soon as I bent over to plant, presenting my back as a feeding platform, they swooped in. In addition, their neighbors joined the festivities and I felt twice as many daggers. I planted the second tree faster than the first. I looked up when I heard Gus yelling "Shit! Fuck!" He was running from one spot to another, jamming trees in the ground like a madman, waving his arms frantically in between. Having no better idea, I adopted his tactic. We worked across the unit, flapping and swatting, running full speed to each spot, cramming trees, and every now and then screaming with helpless rage.

None of this saved us from being drilled by hordes of aerial vampires. You might think the whip-lashed pace would ensure sensational numbers of trees going in the ground, but a mammal only carries so much blood. We worked to the brink of insanity, then fled to the Willys and sat in the cab, chain-smoking dope and drinking warm cans of Coors. As we cowered inside the machine, the mosquitoes lined the periphery of the windows on each door, hundreds of them, smelling our blood and patiently waiting for the chance to quench their thirst. The Willys wasn't airtight, so every now and then one of them would waft in through the floorboards, forcing us to smash it with brutal enthusiasm.

On the second day we worked in forays, running across the unit for an hour or so, until the relentless swarms forced us back to the rig. The heat was intense and prevented us from wearing thicker layers of clothing. There seemed no recourse; we had to finish the contract. Enduring a full day as a blood donor seemed impossible, so we knocked off early and returned to our bug-free base camp, where we sat in the shade, smoking and drinking, hoping to numb the itching. The third day was the same. About halfway through, during yet another spell of hiding in the rig, I argued that we needed to get insect repellant—right now. In those days we never used the stuff, feeling that chemical shields were contrary to the organic tenets of a vague but ardent philosophy about man and nature. At this point, I was more than ready to abandon those convictions.

We drove away to look for a store where we could buy repellant. Unfortunately, it was Sunday, and the only two stores in Priest River were closed. We decided to take the next best option, to drive aimlessly around, drinking beer and enjoying the hot breeze through the open windows of the jeep. The sweet little contract for two was starting to look like another tree planting purgatory. We drove past a golf course, one of those strange leisure parks carved out of the natural landscape and remade in the image of the Scottish moors. We pulled over to savor the incongruity of this refinement amidst the industrial forest. I noticed a shed with several golf carts parked in a line, waiting for their absent masters. On the front rack of every golf cart sat a large can of insect repellant. We laughed and slapped each other's shoulders as if we'd won the lottery. Pillaging the carts, we took several spray cans each, recognizing that our need was primal and took precedence over the sport of golf.

Filled with hope, we drove straight back to the unit and anointed ourselves with the spray until we were greasy and smelled like a chemical factory. It made a difference. But it was still so hot that I sweated off the poison in less than an hour. We stuffed the cans in our tree bags and doused ourselves repeatedly. So much for an organic philosophy. However, we finished the job. No records were set, except for the number of mosquitoes smashed in one blow (fifteen). Rather than glory, we scurried away with relief. Sometimes, that was the best reward.

7

Back to Work

No doubt, if you searched, you could find a first aid kit in the crummy, but I never saw it. I suppose Gus kept it out of sight so he wouldn't have to replenish any used items. That way if an inspector asked to see the kit, a legal requirement for contractors, it was always up to snuff. Given that we were usually hours away from a hospital, if you got seriously hurt, you were probably screwed, anyway.

The only piece of medical equipment we used was a cardboard pallet. Empty seedling boxes could be taken apart and folded into double thickness slabs three feet long. Two of them placed end-to-end made a mattress featuring both insulation and cushioning. Any homeless person can vouch for this versatile end-stage tree product. When we took breaks on hot days, we arranged flattened boxes next to the crummy and sat in the shade, leaning back against the rig as if we were in a lounge.

My first application of cardboard as an emergency treatment happened after I developed an abscessed tooth in the outback of Northern Idaho. The discomfort had been lurking in my jaw for several days, but I tamped it down with beer and weed. One morning, the dull ache erupted into chaotic pain, as if my skull was filled with tiny workers running jackhammers. I couldn't blame it on tree planting, though I wanted to blame it on something besides my own deficient hygiene. It had been years since I'd been to a dentist; in fact, I had previously decided to avoid them altogether. They were sadistic, in my opinion. As a child with bad teeth, I'd had my fill of their peering and probing and the creepy reflectors they wore on their heads. I rejected the lectures, and all the claptrap cautions about cuspids and whatnot. However, there's nothing like throbbing pain to undermine pompous ideals.

After trying to plant some trees, I gave up and stumbled back to the rig. Laying some cardboard on the gravel, I threw myself on the pallet. Writhing and moaning ensued. The crummy was the only transport off the unit and it wasn't going anywhere till the end of the workday. So, I lay there, wallowing in the pathetic agony of my plight. The performance lead to a variety of supportive comments from the crew, such as "What the fuck is wrong with you?" and "Dude, you don't look good." No reply was possible or expected as they stepped around me, going about their work as if I wasn't dying a shitty death on a dirt road in hell.

We didn't have health insurance in those days. I didn't even know what it was. We just suffered until it got so bad you went to a doctor and forked over the cash. Clearly, I was at that point, so when we returned to camp, I drank myself to sleep, and the next morning drove my truck to the nearest town big enough to harbor a dentist. I begged the receptionist for an immediate intervention. She consulted with the dentist, and he agreed, although

I must have been a daunting sight: long, greasy hair, shredded clothes, unwashed, ungroomed, the sasquatch in person. Within minutes, I was shown to the chair. I don't remember if he used anesthetic. Maybe not. He grappled the bad tooth with some kind of industrial tongs and pulled and pulled, putting his whole body into it. I swear he had a foot braced against the chair. It felt like he was removing my jaw with a wrecking bar. Moans and howls of pain escaped my mouth as the offending tooth finally gave up its unwelcome residence. I'm sure they heard it in the waiting room. When I walked out everyone stared at me as if I had risen from the dead. The procedure felt barbaric and was certainly excruciating but the relief was prompt, for which I was thankful. I happily surrendered my cash and drove into the woods, straight to the unit, and got back to work.

The following year we were back in Idaho, once again suffering through the heat of late spring and early summer. The crisp, dry air sucked the moisture out of both seedlings and planters. One afternoon when the temperature hit 104 degrees, I took a break at the crummy. I felt weak and nauseous. Standing next to the rig, I put my hand on the open door to steady myself. Lester looked up from the gold pan where he was rolling a joint and offered advice: "Man, you should lay down."

I knew something was wrong because I didn't even want to smoke the joint. I felt suddenly drained of life energy, like a ghost. I spread out some cardboard and sprawled on it. In the sun, though, because I was shivering with chills. At various points, crew members would stand over me and offer suggestions. Somebody encouraged me to drink water. I guess we had water, although I don't know why, I only remember having oranges and beer in the crummy. I spent the rest of that day on the pallet, like in the song by Mississippi John Hurt: "make me a pallet down, soft and low/make me a pallet on your floor." I drifted in and out of consciousness in a blues delirium. After the crew's work was done, they took me back to camp and I slept straight through to the next morning. When I woke up, I thought I could go back to work, so I did. Whatever happened the day before was forgotten. Later I found out that I had the symptoms of heat exhaustion. If I hadn't spent the day on cardboard, soft and low, I might have advanced to heat stroke and died right on the damned unit.

Disasters engulfed the whole crew at times. During my first season, we woke up one morning to hurricane force winds. The Forest Service drove up to the unit and told us to get the hell out of the woods. I didn't blame them, the trees around the edge of the clear cut were dancing like wild men, straining to flex into yoga poses as the wind howled at their resistance. This was the early days of the crew and we'd camped on the unit. I had my sturdy mountain tent tucked under some old growth Douglas Fir along the margin of the cut. Since it was a two-person tent, I'd been sharing it with Lester. It was fun; we swapped sarcastic rejoinders at bedtime and snored at each other all night. The tent was sturdy enough to endure ferocious mountain gales, and I left it standing as we followed the Forest Service directive to leave the woods. Lester offered his log cabin in Newport as a refuge, about an hour away. The whole crew went there and sat around smoking, drinking, and bullshitting while his wife Roberta acted like she didn't mind. Their five kids treated it like a party, stealing sips of beer and running around the house yelling. After observing the family dynamics for a while, I wasn't surprised that Lester chose to stay in my tent instead of commuting home.

Two days later, Roberta had stopped talking and wore a permanent scowl. The winds finally faded, and Gus was anxious to get back to making money, so we piled into the trucks and drove off. Roberta managed a tight smile and waved us away with a dish towel. Back at the unit, Lester and I found a three-foot diameter fir tree lying flat across the tent. The wind had ripped the tree out by the roots, just like my tooth, in another epic struggle. The ridge line of the tent was crushed, and the fabric blown apart like an explosion. A thick, broken branch stabbed down through the tent floor and into the earth underneath, on Lester's side, right where his upper torso would have been. We stood there and looked at the tent in a slack-jawed stupor, lost in our own thoughts about the whims of fortune. It added a strange bond to our friendship, as if we had shared a near-death experience, which in a way, we had. Lester took it personally and talked for days about that branch: "right through my heart!"

The tent was trashed beyond repair, and I spent the rest of the contract sleeping under a tarp. As for Lester, he decided that commuting back and forth to his home wasn't so bad.

Since we had neoprene rain gear and were supposed to be tough as nails, we usually ignored the weather. Not that we had any say over the atmosphere; we just flipped up the jacket hood and pushed on. Typically, it was the Forest Service and their liability concerns that intervened between our work and the weather. Only once do I remember a shutdown originating with the crew. It happened in Northern Idaho as thunderstorms roiled overhead in the late spring heat. The heavens rumbled and darkened; I waited for the deluge of rain. Nearby thunder blasts kept us nervous. I kept stopping and looking around, as if I could see it before it happened. I glanced toward the ridge at the top of the unit during one of these scans and saw a huge Ponderosa Pine take a direct hit from a bolt of lightning. I was looking right at it as the bolt struck. It flamed into a towering roman candle, filling me with an awe that two heart beats later transformed into fear. The strike was only two hundred yards away—too close for comfort. Here we were, out in the middle of a large open area, swinging metal hoedads over our heads. It didn't sit right, so I yelled at the boss. "Gus! Is this safe?" He shrugged. I broadcast the same question to the rest of the crew. None of them thought it was safe. Reluctantly, Gus agreed to retreat. The pine tree, despite its spectacular flame, had flared out after the fire rushed up the trunk.

A couple hours later, when the storm had passed, we drove up the hill to inspect the tree and make sure we didn't have a budding forest fire burning us out of a job. Its roots still smoldered, so we dumped water and shoveled dirt. A magnificent tree, it had reigned over this spot for hundreds of years. Despite the drama of the lightning strike, the tree appeared undamaged except for some charred bark and a loss of needles, gone in the flash flame. Trees can survive such things, but there was no sense in letting it smolder underground and weaken the roots. Nobody knew how to fight forest fires, we just reacted instinctively. Check the tree and render first aid. This action later earned us a fire pay bonus from the Forest Service, a welcome tip of the hat from our frequent adversaries.

The next day, of course, it was back to work.

8

A Society of Sorts

What started out as a temporary job in the woods developed into a society with its own culture. The value patterns we had learned as children were reshuffled or abandoned in the social turmoil of the 70s. We pushed the limits, often heedless, headless, and downright stupid, all in the name of being free. Running away from social norms didn't encourage a reasoned approach to where we were going. One thing led to another; a lot of shit happened without decisions.

But even as we played at freedom, it turned out that we didn't know how to live beyond social conventions. Trends of normalcy crept back in. Nothing demonstrated that more than our changing base camp accommodations. The Swinging Hoedads may have started as a cluster of barbarians sleeping under machines and sheets of plastic, but time transformed us into a nomadic band of families adapting to the challenges of migrant work.

During the first two years, a visitor to our camp would have seen the squalor typical of the industrial forest: a landing with battered pickups and a car or two, half-collapsed umbrella tents, wet socks, scattered gloves, and orange peels strewn around the gravel. Off to the side, a campfire ring. Near that you'd find a fire-blackened cooking pot with food remains burnt into the creases. A discarded seedling box full of crumpled beer cans. And propped against a rock, a trenching tool for urgent missions into the woods. In short, hearth and kitchen as envisioned by men in a feral condition.

We accepted the crude arrangements for a while, but when we started to see ourselves as a working crew and that tree planting was our job, not just a macho lark, then the sleaze became harder to tolerate. The job was tough enough—perhaps having a few comforts wasn't unreasonable. So, we got serious about being professionals. The camps began to show improvements with better tents, propane stoves for cooking, five-gallon water jugs, tarps strung from trucks and trees to create dry space, folding tables and chairs, kitchenware, and even cleaning supplies. One year a new crew member drove to base in a pickup with a cab-over camper and it was clear that needless austerity was a thing of the past.

Working in the woods had traditionally been the business of men. Women couldn't handle the work, said the men who knew. As for living in the primitive conditions, women wouldn't put up with it. This reasoning, if you can call it that, ignored the million or more years that our ancestors lived together—men, women, and children—in far more primitive situations. Despite the rustic circumstances of the tree planting world and our biases, it didn't take long before we wanted to bring our partners, girlfriends, or wives for companionship. I don't think any of us thought that there would be a benefit for these women. Maybe they'd be better positioned to understand our tall tales—if that's a benefit. No, it was mostly because we were tired of sleeping alone and eating our own cooking.

When I went to work with Gus for the first tree planting season, my partner Debby stayed home. We agreed that it was prudent, even if it wasn't going to be easy for her. Our primitive shack had no electricity or indoor plumbing, and was situated about three miles outside of a junction in the road named Mazama. The town contained a small Post Office with a single gas pump. Set in a wide valley flanked by soaring mountains and dense forest, it was an idyllic setting with barely a hint of civilization. I left her the old Chevy pickup, so she'd have a shot at survival, and I hitch-hiked to Spokane. I didn't know how long I'd be gone or what I was getting into. Once I'd started the job, it took over. No way could I quit, leave Gus in the lurch, and abandon the crew. Or so I told myself.

Being a captive in the industrial forest, I was cut off from everything else going on in my life. I'd like to say that I wrote Debby a letter or two, describing all the intense new experiences and my piles of wealth. But I don't know if I even wrote one letter, let alone two. We never left the job except when the Forest Service shut us down for high winds. And then we only went as far as Lester's home in the lowlands where we lay around drinking beer and annoying his wife. Going to a post office and sending a card or letter didn't cross my mind. I can't explain that; it's not like I didn't think about her. Perhaps it was a sign of how far my world had shrunk, from a globe to a unit, to a bag of trees, to the next hole in the ground.

Planting season that year lasted about two months, and when it ended, I realized it was time to go home. It was like waking up and remembering you had a life somewhere else, somewhere that didn't involve clear cuts. I looked forward to the warm welcome I would receive from Debby after the prolonged absence. When Gus dropped me outside the Spokane city limits to hitchhike, I was eager to get home.

I remember standing by the side of the road, sticking out my thumb for every car; there weren't many. I was tired and dirty, wearing my tree planting clothes, but I had a two thousand dollar check in my pocket, a weird dissonance. Taking a bus never crossed my mind; they didn't go to Mazama. I waited for an hour or so, enjoying the warm sun, reveling in the knowledge that I wouldn't have to get up the next day and plant more trees. Eventually, a convertible sports car pulled over and ended my reverie. It was a woman driver, an astonishing situation. Women were usually too cautious to take the risk of picking up hitchhikers. I didn't blame them, not one bit. I ran to the convertible and saw that the driver was young, with a mane of long, curly blond hair. She asked where I was going and didn't blink an eye when I named a town hundreds of miles away on back roads. "We'll get you there," she smiled. I wedged my pack behind the seats, and jumped in. The car was small and sporty. She said it was a Fiat Spider; I'd never seen one. We chatted a bit on the road, but before long she pulled over. "I'm exhausted; could you drive?" Could I? A sports car with the top down? I could, and did, while the woman snoozed. Every now and then I'd glance over and marvel at her trusting nature. She was beautiful like an angel, taking me in one swoop to my destination, a miracle on the highway.

We drove five hours across the flatlands of Eastern Washington, before I finally pulled in at our cabin. I'll never forget the expression on Debby's face as she stepped through the door and saw the Fiat, me behind the wheel, and the movie starlet by my side. She recovered quickly and acted like my flamboyant return was the norm. Later, after the angel left, we talked. She accepted my excuses for not writing, but when the next tree planting season approached, she announced that she was coming, too. She did, and she wasn't the only woman curious to see what was going on out in the woods.

After Debby came Mary, wife of Joe, another recruit from the Spokane commune. Soon she and Debby were best friends, clinging to each other out of necessity as well as affinity. Once the gender barrier of tree planting camp was broken, Gus brought his wife, Cathy. These three women took over all matters not involving trees and drugs.

Cathy, who was no fool, pressured Gus until he purchased an army surplus field tent to serve as a base. A brown canvas monster fifteen feet wide and thirty feet long, it was the heaviest tent on earth and took spirited effort to set up, but once up, it provided formidable shelter. The tent came with an insulation liner and a roof gasket for a stovepipe. Solid enough to endure serious weather, on hot days the sides could be rolled up for air with the option of lowering bug-proof mesh panels. The whole thing had the drab chic of military style, but we loved it. It offered reliable shelter, warmth, and respite from whatever was going on in the great outdoors. With room for counters, shelves, folding chairs, tables, and so forth, it quickly became domestic. We dubbed it the "Big Tent." It served as the center of operations for the women, and they managed it with ruthless authority, snarling and snapping at anyone getting in their way or acting like it was a barn instead of a home.

With this approximation of domesticity, we assumed the roles predetermined by our parents and their society. The men planted trees and the women cooked. In the mid-70s, most of the men I knew were stuck in a frontier ethos, or some imaginary understanding of the frontier. We'd grown up on a heavy diet of western movies where men were men and women were not. An excess of psychedelic drugs blurred these stereotypes into the strange, hippie blend of art nouveau and the Old West, but not much changed. Chicks were in the kitchen, man; they knew about that stuff. Men were the gunslingers, firing as many trees into the ground as we could, hoedad blades hot with vigor. Even though the gendered bullshit was thick, the old ladies accepted the task of taking care of their old men. Every day we returned from work to large quantities of hot food and a warm hearth, and we embraced it. Women never planted for The Swinging Hoedads. Not that I recall any of the women saying they wanted to plant trees. Given the prospect of hanging around with us all day or staying in camp with the other women, I can't say that I blame them.

Tree-planting money, all two or three months of it, was supposed to carry us through the rest of the year. It never did, but after my third season, flush with some cash, Debby and I made a down payment on a piece of undeveloped land several miles away in the hills above Mazama. It was only accessible on a long string of rutted dirt roads during the summer and early fall. When the snow fell, any time after Halloween, the roads became impassable and would remain that way for almost six months. For some reason this seemed quaint and appealing. It certainly reduced the cost of the land. As soon as the planting work was done the following year, we moved to our seventeen acres, set up a tent, and started building a log cabin. It took all summer but cost only $300 for the materials we couldn't salvage from the surrounding woods. Because we owned it, we lived there for a few years, fashioning a lifestyle best described as close to the bone.

Outside of tree planting in the spring, odd jobs with the neighbors, and unemployment benefits, we had no income. Sometimes we barely got by. Our mainstay was the fifty-pound bag of pinto beans stashed in a garbage can. Despite the fluctuations of income, we settled into predictable cycles, mostly dictated by the seasons. Over the summer, I worked on upgrading the cabin, growing a vegetable or two, cultivating marijuana, and gathering firewood. In winter, there wasn't much besides cross-country skiing and reading Russian novels. Cabin life was soothing, but right after a season of tree planting, I needed downtime to wring out all the intensity of the work and readjust to the rhythm of country life. Typically, I sat in a daze for a week or more, sleeping most of the time. As soon as I found some motivation, I started picking away at projects that needed to be done during the summer and before the heavy snows of winter. By heavy I mean a consistent three-to-four-foot snowpack. When the snow melted in early spring, the start date of tree planting season loomed, darkening the remaining days of freedom. The long dreams of winter suddenly seemed more precious, not to be squandered. I dreaded the plunge back into tree planting frenzy, but it was the only way I knew how to make money.

Despite the meditative nature of living in an isolated mountain cabin, it fostered a penetrating loneliness. No one came to visit in winter. The nearest snow-plowed parking area was two miles away and a thousand feet down the hill. We made the trek once a week on skis just to go to town and get supplies, an all-day activity. Whatever we got had to be packed or sledded back up the snow-covered road, always a workout. Neither of us flourished in those conditions. After the first winter on the land, as soon as we reunited with the Swinging Hoedads in spring, we extolled the beauty of our seventeen acres, emphasizing how much room there was for others. Eventually, Joe and Mary took the bait. We helped them build a cabin and suddenly, it wasn't so lonely.

Most of the crew had similar lifestyles. We owned little pieces of land out in the boonies, strewn from the North Cascades across to Montana. We all hibernated through snowy winters, and reconvened every spring to replant the industrial forest. When we started having kids, we brought them to work, too. The little wild things began to fill the nooks and corners of camp, running around in the dirt and gravel, playing with sticks and stones for toys. Several kids were born on the job, in campers and tents, birthed in dramatic urgency and with a naive confidence in the ways of nature. My own first-born son came into the world in Lester's log cabin in Northeastern Washington. By the light of kerosene lamps, Debby pushed him out into the receiving hands of the other women. It was an auspicious moment for me, on the first day of summer while a lightning storm boomed a welcome to the world. Giddy with the signs, we named him Sampsa after the character from Finnish mythology, a folk hero who planted so many trees that they grew to cover the world in forest.

As if imbued with the energy of that mythic hero, on my first day back at work I set a blistering pace. When I told Gus that I'd planted over 1600 trees in less than six hours, he looked at me with skepticism. But we never lied about tree count; it was a knight's honor kind of thing. Finally, he smiled and said: "I should give everybody a day off to have kids."

Other children born to the crew ended up with names like Leaf, Cedar, Oceana, and Meadow, nomenclature that reflected our desire to see the primal forces of the world prosper in the face of human exploitation. I doubt there were advantages to growing up in tree-planting camps, but the presence of the kids, perhaps more than anything else, provided a sense that we were something more than your average work crew.

Although the intensity of reforestation labor had eroded our delusions of sylvan idealism, the fantasies were tenacious, and resurfaced in a hardier form as we became a tree-planting band. As we learned to work the job and develop a professional identity, we also embodied a counterculture, which meant that it wasn't just a job, it was a lifestyle, with women, children, a mythology, and a kit full of tools to perform the task. Living in the woods, working off the grid and out of the mainstream, we did a dirty job considered by most in the forestry business to be untouchable. It was as if we'd taken on a holy mission to regenerate the woods obliterated by the corporate world. I often told myself such things, high as a kite, when I needed to balance the grim days of exhaustion. But there were still too many things wrong with the scene for me to entirely believe my own hogwash. I thought I was plenty cynical about it all, certainly enough to disavow any naivete. When the next lesson came, it was rude. Working for the National Forest gave us a benevolent niche where our supervisors were tolerant; hardly the cruel masters we made them out to be. When we emerged from the National Forests to tackle the private landowners, the big time of tree planting, I would learn how sheltered I'd been.

9

Capitalist Roadkill

Rolling through unit after unit, the success of our planting techniques went to our heads; you'd need a bulldozer to flatten the hubris. It was our destiny to reforest the world and not only that, we'd do it our way. We begged Gus to find more work and expand the season; we promised to go anywhere. Taking us at our word, he signed a contract with Weyerhaeuser Company to plant some of their low elevation land on the Olympic Peninsula. We welcomed the job; it meant we could work all winter. Plus, this was private industry: the Big Time. If things went well, there'd be no end to the work.

Weyerhaeuser is the world's largest private owner and manager of timberland. Between the US and Canada alone, they control over 26 million acres. Under various names, they've been at the resource exploitation game for a long time, predating the existence of the US Forest Service. In 1900, the Great Northern Railroad sold Friedrich Weyerhaeuser almost a million acres of prime Washington timberland, land that had been granted by the federal government to the railroad as an incentive for its construction. Weyerhaeuser was a notorious robber baron with a history of anti-trust violations. His company immediately set to work replicating reliable patterns of generating wealth. Since then, the company has clear cut four million acres of American forest. Without irony, they now call themselves "the tree-growing company," making a noisy display of their demonstration tree farms and their commitment to a self-interested notion of sustainability. Many of the trees originally cut from their Washington land featured specimens hundreds of years old and irreplaceable on a capitalist-driven timetable. They had no intention of sustaining these old growth forests; there's no money in it. Weyerhaeuser's idea of sustainability revolves around forty-to-sixty-year harvest cycles, adequate for pulp and cheap framing lumber. You can forget about the fine-grained, beautiful wood of mature trees; it's gone.

Before corporate logging, the Olympic rain forest supported astonishing ecologies of old growth trees, moss, and lichens, all interwoven into a complex web of life. You can still see that ecosystem in the national park and other protected areas. Not so much on private land, however; that's been converted to second growth and brush. Second growth trees still comprise a forest, but it's a forest managed as a monoculture, like a field of corn or wheat, lacking in the rich, wild diversity created over time. When you walk through these woods, they feel barren.

For the Weyerhauser job, we rented cabins next to the ocean because camping out in the winter rain forest seemed too masochistic even for us. Situated just behind the dune line between the woods and the beach, the cabins comprised a sad cluster of shacks built for summer tourists. Exposed to every storm blowing off the Pacific, these basic huts fostered tides of mold in the penetrating humidity. Still, they provided shelter from the constant lashing of wind and rain. Those of us who had families had the distraction of partners and children to offset the sixteen hours of darkness. A heated space and daily showers, it was alarmingly civilized, like we'd sold out to the corporate life. As I waited for the crummy each morning, I sat at the small kitchen table, glancing through the misty window panes while smoking a joint and reading *Finnegans Wake*, a page a day, the only book crazy enough for the job.

Driving to the planting site for the first time, we learned that Weyerhaeuser required work crews to wear hard hats. Fuck that, we didn't own hard hats or have any desire to own hard hats. Gus, in his benevolence, revealed that he had known about this all along and had taken the initiative to bring a box of them, anticipating that we would have figured out some way to sabotage if we'd known about it. I selected a silver colored, brimmed dome like the one worn by the Roman god Mercury. I put it on and buckled the chin strap; it wasn't heavy. I did not, however, feel any safer.

Sporting our tin pots, we milled around outside the crummy, meeting the inspector and surveying the unit. It was enormous, perhaps two hundred flat, scalped acres where we were the tallest living things. After a brief discussion of how we would float the unit, we bagged up trees and wandered off. There would be no root trimming or vermiculite sloughing here; the inspector watched us like a hawk. This was their land, their trees, their investment, and there would be good regeneration or else. We could live with that, we wanted the trees to grow anyway, so off we went.

It didn't take long for the inspector to freak out. Weyerhaeuser was used to traditional tree planting crews that ran in lines and ate up ground in contiguous swaths. The inspector would follow along behind these crews, digging up trees and promptly broadcasting the results to the foreman so the crew could tighten up the spacing, cut out the J roots, and plant better trees. When our inspector saw us fan out in different directions, planting all over the place in what seemed to be random chaos, he ran to Gus with a litany of complaints. He didn't know where to start digging. He didn't know how he could get us to fix the mistakes. He didn't think we could cover the ground without missing spots. Gus waved a few of us over to join the conversation. We asked him if he had found any problems with the trees. No. We asked him if he found missed spots in our planting. No, spacing was tight. We'd run into this resistance with the Forest Service, so we patiently explained our method, and how it would, indeed, cover the ground thoroughly, we're just floating this area and that area like so, see? He didn't see. He walked across the unit trying to find trees to dig and looked exasperated because he couldn't understand our stoner relationship with the terrain. When we said we were floating, I'm sure he thought we were talking about something else.

He became a contemptible character in our eyes, a real straight arrow, and a bit of a dandy. He would pause from his wandering and digging to lean on the shovel, scanning the horizon for crazed hippies. When he didn't think anyone was watching, he would pull a comb out of his pocket, take off his hard hat, and comb his hair with deliberate precision, making sure that each modest hair was in its place. We were amazed; we considered inspectors to be a weird lot, but most of them accepted that you get mussed up walking around in dirt and debris all day; some of them even seemed to get a kick out of getting down with the dirt dog tree planters. But this guy—I've never seen a man spend so much time on his hair; he went through this routine every hour.

We cast him as the villain in our mythic melodrama. Relentlessly, he accosted us at the landing, whining about our planting formations and how we needed to start working closer together. Usually, Gus was the target of this nonsense, and Gus dutifully relayed these concerns to the crew, with no attempt to influence our response; he knew better.

This back and forth went on for weeks. In my head, I thought the company should be kissing our asses, grateful that they were getting the job done and done well. But that's not the corporate way. We were out of line, doing our own thing, whatever it was. The whining and complaining continued. I let the inspector's tiresome performance get under my skin. One day I lost it and threw my hoedad at him. It's a good thing that it didn't connect, because it could have been lethal, especially if it caught him without his hard hat. I was below the road, down a small incline while he strutted above, broadcasting the usual corporate guidance to the lackeys toiling in the soil. I screamed incoherently and hurled the hoedad up to the road. It sailed over the berm and out of sight. He must have scurried away, because when I got up to the landing the hoedad was laying on the road and he was nowhere to be seen, having retreated to his truck and left the unit.

He didn't report it to the sheriff, which he had every right to do. I guess he understood we didn't like his supervision. Of course, in the rough and tumble woods culture of the Northwest, it wasn't uncommon for men to go off the rails in anger about one thing or another and express themselves in unfortunate behaviors. This is one of the reasons why a woods worker was sometimes called a "timber beast." You could get red suspenders in the local mercantile with just that slogan printed vertically in bold black letters, one word on each suspender, just in case you wanted to dispel any questions about who or what you were and why you shouldn't be fucked with. I guess I thought I was one, but I felt ashamed of my act, anyway. I didn't really want to kill the guy; I just wanted him to go away.

Not long after this incident we were called to a meeting with the Weyerhaeuser bigwigs. They really summoned Gus, because in corporate culture managers only want to deal with other managers, not peons. But Gus had no interest in speaking for his crew, so he invited me, Lester, and Joe to accompany him. He'd done his best to be a bridge of reason between Weyerhaeuser and the Swinging Hoedads, but he was no doubt tired of trying to explain us to them or them to us. He was sly how he coaxed me to join him for the meeting. I had certainly been one of the loudest and most frequent complainers about "this goddam Weyerhaeuser bullshit" and I had given myself permission to rant in full color when it came to the subject. Gus lured me into the posse by saying that it was necessary to have someone speak with lyricism about the situation and "we need your poetic voice and vision." Sucked me right in, the clever man.

We parked in front of a large office building on the outskirts of a nearby town. I had no idea where Weyerhaeuser's central office was located, they probably owned a city of gold somewhere. This was just the local headquarters for their holdings on the Olympic Peninsula. As we got out of the crummy, I felt nervous. For all my willingness to perform in front of the home crowd, I knew I was far out of my element. The shiny new building towered over us, emphasizing that we were just a ragtag band of miscreants. We walked through the front doors and were dirtier than anything in the building, even though we'd made an effort to dress in our best. Basically, we didn't have a best. All we had were the clothes we worked in, and since that's where we were going after the meeting, that's what we had on.

A well-groomed secretary ushered us into a large office. Two guys said hello and introduced themselves, identifying their roles as field supervisors. They wore jeans, flannel work shirts, Buffalo boots, and red suspenders, all fresh and clean. The suspenders did not identify them as timber beasts. In fact, I didn't for a minute believe these guys ever stepped outside the office, though if they did, they had the correct look. They indicated we could sit in plastic chairs while one of them perched on the edge of his desk and the other draped an arm over a free-standing white board. In alternating paragraphs, they launched into an explanation of "the Weyerhaeuser Way" as if they were giving a Sunday school class about the stone tablets handed directly to Friedrich Weyerhaeuser himself.

We listened to the timber geeks lecture, then we tried to explain ourselves. We described our floating method of covering ground in plain, simple words, enumerating the advantages. I drew some diagrams on the whiteboard so they could understand it even better. We extolled the efficiency of our method, even to the point of bragging. They listened with noncommittal expressions, but it soon became obvious that they weren't interested in our lunatic hippie ideas. Their priority was how easy it was going to be for their employee, the inspector, to do *his* job. They didn't care about our brilliant methods. We were contractors, of no concern to them, and we were hired to do the job their way or we weren't going to be doing it, period. Far from a negotiation, this was an ultimatum.

I tried to be poetic or lyrical or whatever the hell Gus was expecting, but it fell on prosaic ears. It was clear that we, like every other planting crew they hired, were expected to work the Weyerhaeuser way. Chastised, we trooped out of the fancy office building and back to our stupid old crummy. We rolled a joint to dispel the gloom. I chafed at my failure to win a poetic victory in the heart of corporate America, and I fell into a terrible sulk that lasted for days.

Finally, I got up one morning, and told Debby I couldn't do it anymore. She'd been listening to me complain for weeks and just nodded. We packed the pickup, tucked our young son into his car seat, and headed back to our mountain cabin. We stopped by the unit so I could say goodbye to the crew. This was the first time I had walked out on a job, and I felt a little sad. However, no one shed any tears. I don't remember it, but Joe assured me later that as I drove away, I called out the window: "see ya later, suckers!" Only there was no later; I'd planted my last tree with the Swinging Hoedads.

10

A Brief Career in Espionage

Tree planting with the Swinging Hoedads had been a show without an audience. Our melodramas were staged amidst the ghosts of vanished trees, far from public awareness. Outside the blurred succession of our contracts, I had a sketchy understanding of what went on in the world of reforestation. We'd heard Lester's tales about other contractors with their screaming foremen and lockstep crews. The Weyerhaeuser experience provided another window into that world, but I'd seen enough. As for what else was out there, who knew? Seven years into my tree-planting career I'd never met a planter that didn't work for Gus.

When I walked off the Weyerhaeuser job, I had no plan. Worn down by the corporate imperative for conformity and by tree planting in general, I felt drained of purpose. I hadn't intended to quit the Swinging Hoedads, but I needed a break. Gus had put up with my hyperbolic raving for years, and despite my proclamation, I know he still considered me an asset. Not long after Debby and I got back to our cabin, I received a letter from him. He asked—since I had nothing else to do—if I'd represent the crew at a tree planting conference. I was intrigued. A tree planting conference, who knew such things existed? I'd been in hiding from the world for a while, either within the container of the industrial forest or the isolated realm of our North Cascades home. I avoided gatherings, groups, parties, and organizations, but something about this conference triggered my curiosity. I agreed to go.

Gus sent me a packet of material, and I studied it closely. The conference was the annual meeting of a group called the Northwest Forest Workers Association. Their ambition was to organize tree planters into a trade association with union-like power, an echo of old syndicalist ideas. As I studied their history, I learned that a large group of tree planters in Eugene had formed a reforestation cooperative in the early 70s named simply The Hoedads. I wondered if Gus had known about them when he named his crew but decided that any resemblance was probably a coincidence. After all, a hoedad was the signature tool of the job. It seemed that the Oregon Hoedads weren't a monolithic organization; they operated multiple crews in a loose federation under a unified financial umbrella. I read through the amusing list of crew names: Mudsharks, Red Star, Natural Wonders, PF Flyers, Homegrown, and Different Strokes were a few examples. A feminist vanguard had established a women-only crew called Full Moon Rising. Although I'd never seen a woman plant trees, I knew that there had to be a few who could handle it. A whole crew of them struck me as improbable, but I had a lot to learn.

The Hoedad crews may have represented diverse interests, but they were singular with their politics. Crews governed themselves by an inclusive democratic process, without bosses. Then, in 1976, The Hoedads conglomerate allied with two other reforestation cooperatives, another Oregon outfit named Green Side Up, and one from Seattle called Marmot Construction Works. These crews formed the Northwest Forest Workers Association, NWFWA ("noofwah"). Their mission to organize grew out of a radical tradition that dated back to the days of the IWW. By the time I finished studying the conference packet, I understood that these people were grounded in history and serious.

The 1980 NWFWA conference took place mid-winter on Marrowstone Island in Puget Sound, hosted by Marmot. As I digested what I'd learned, I knew that I had to attend; it sounded almost too good to be true. The conference agenda addressed sensible topics like worker safety and health, the inherent antagonisms of contracting, the science and politics of forestry management, and the difficulties in promoting worker solidarity—all that interspersed with music, dancing, and food. None of this interested Gus, except perhaps the food; he was suspicious of political organization, especially something calling itself a trade association. I'm not sure why he wanted me to go; he probably guessed that it would only exacerbate my idealism.

As a teenager I'd wanted nothing more than to be a Red; if I could have grown a beard it would have been a Bolshevik goatee. I read a lot of history for a kid my age. As soon as I started learning about it, I latched onto the socialist paradigm of a worker's paradise. Not that I knew anything about work; I only had a paper route and sometimes mowed the neighbor's lawn. Still, the drama and purpose of revolutionary rhetoric populated my fantasies. None of this idealism filtered into anything practical. Yet I carried it with me as I graduated from high school, dropped out of college, and became a bum. I managed to survive without a regular job until I started tree planting. Of course, that wasn't very regular. But it was a job, which made me an actual worker.

The years of laboring on Gus's contracts provoked a lot of questions about what we were doing. Even though Gus was a good friend, I found myself rebelling against the benevolent patriarch. He didn't dominate the crew, he truly embodied a live and let live philosophy, but he kept the business end of the business to himself. Occasionally Lester or I would be asked to provide input on scouting new contracts, giving him the benefit of our opinions on what it would take to get the job done, but beyond that I didn't know much. The expertise and competence of the crew allowed Gus to make astute bids, winning jobs over contractors who worked from a general template or higher overhead. He paid us five dollars an hour at the end of the season, and we gave a big chunk of it right back to him to cover the advances for food and dope, not that I blame him for that. After a couple of years, I remember getting bumped up to six bucks. Due to my ignorance of the working world, I had no way of evaluating the wage. Perhaps Gus should have paid us more, but we didn't care, at least not at first.

Uncertain about my role in the Swinging Hoedads and curious to see how other crews worked, I went to the NWFWA conference hoping to learn about ways to improve our operations. I don't know what I was thinking, really, probably something along the lines of "sowing the seeds of revolt" and other slogans I'd picked up from reading labor history. However, I was too shy to be a revolutionary. When I drove to the state park conference center and introduced myself at the registration desk, I was welcomed by the Marmot hosts, but quickly swallowed up in a crowd of a hundred people. Everyone seemed to know everyone else, and the laughter and chat enhanced my tendency to withdraw.

I tried to blend in and look like I belonged, but I clung to the margins. Unfortunately, the groups sat in big circles, a configuration that left me feeling exposed. As I listened to lectures and discussions, I appreciated the dedication of the participants. The Hoedad contingent seemed full of earnest young men who wanted to change the world and were keen to speak at length on the subject. During the well-attended presentation about contracting, one of these fellows, a guy wearing a Chairman Mao cap with a red star emblem, cautioned the audience to be very careful in discussing bidding strategies. He said there was an industrial spy at the conference. I couldn't imagine such a thing. As he stared in my direction, I realized that he meant me. I was stunned, and instantly ashamed. I'd been soaking up the utopian scene like it was a film by Warren Beatty and did not appreciate how real it was for some folks. After being called out, I sat, paralyzed, at the center of everyone's attention. It would have been a good time to vanish in a puff of smoke, had I known how. Mortified and panicky, I stammered out a declaration of solidarity or something to that effect. I'm sure I cut a pathetic figure. Several folks, including some Marmots who had made the original invitation, stood up for my right to be there. Still, it was a rude awakening into the torment of radical process. Marmot had taken the initiative to invite the Swinging Hoedads, perhaps out of a spirit of inclusion or an evangelical gesture, or maybe just to check us out. But not everybody wanted to see a running dog capitalist sniffing around the inner sanctum.

The situation helped put Gus' actions in perspective. He had consistently underbid The Hoedads and other contractors trying to get work in the Spokane area, and they didn't like it. His bids were low, sometimes so low they seemed unbelievable to these organizations. Not surprising, given their overhead (it can be expensive to fund equality). I understood the dilemma: workplace economy doesn't always mesh with social justice goals. Regardless, at the time of the conference, as I sat on the cusp of two worlds trying to sort out my own priorities, I resented the accusation of vile intentions. Any righteous anger I might have summoned couldn't break through the veil of shame, though. Maybe I should have been flattered, because it's not every day you get to be a spy. But I only wanted to slink away.

I took a lot of notes at the conference. No trade secrets, though, nothing to bury the socialist tree planters in their own duff. Instead, my notes were filled with dreamy poetry and ecstatic praise for the views from the Marrowstone beach. When I needed to escape the social melee, I walked a hundred yards to the shore where with a simple turn of the head I could see two snow-capped mountain ranges and the island-strewn waters of Puget Sound revealed in sparkling winter sunshine. I also wrote about the members of the Marmot collective. Half of them were women. Strong and confident, these were empowered feminists, women who expected respect and equality as a matter of course. I was more than a little in awe. All the Marmots I met, both women and men, exhibited personal warmth and camaraderie.

They seemed to glow with vigor. And from the guys, I didn't sense any of the usual macho bullshit.

After the conference, as we rode back on the ferry, one of the Marmot women asked me, "So what do you think of us?" I looked at her, with her beret and unadorned beauty and thought she was like every radical boy's dream of a rebel girl. My thoughts drifted to the namesake animal of the collective, a favorite creature of mine, and I told her that everyone seemed "warm and fuzzy." I meant it as praise, but she didn't like it, and frowned, seeing herself, and her comrades, as tough and competent. And maybe they were, but at the time I craved warm and fuzzy. I needed to believe in something bigger than being a hard ass gunslinger of the woods. Marmot personalities hinted that a working identity could be more complex. Somehow, they'd grafted eager ideals onto a basic pragmatism. I wanted to know more about that.

Marmot's ease of togetherness and solidarity struck me as more profound than anything I had experienced. The moments of team synchronicity I'd felt with Swinging Hoedads seemed superficial in comparison. Marmots didn't just see the next unit, they were looking at life, at "rebuilding society within the shell of the old," just like the anarchist creed. I left the NWFWA conference giddy, as if I was in love. When I reported back to Gus, since I had no trade secrets to share, I asked him if he would be willing to reorganize as a co-op. He wasn't. This didn't surprise me, so I told him I wouldn't be coming back. My mind was clear. It was time for a change. I went home and mailed an application to Marmot Construction Works.

11

Down the Marmot Hole

A month later, I arrived for an interview at the Marmot office in Seattle, swallowing my nerves like lumps of stale bread. I stepped inside the weathered storefront on Capitol Hill to find a long, narrow room, silent. Waiting for someone to respond to my entrance, I shuffled, cleared my throat, and tried a modest "Hello?" I heard noises from the back, through an open door, otherwise nothing. The walls were lined with shelves sagging under tools and gear. I knew Marmot did timber thinning and trail construction as well as tree planting and I wasn't surprised to see everything from chainsaws to rock bars. All the tools carried the patina of heavy use. The office resembled a garage more than an office, although amidst the clutter I identified a battered metal desk, a few filing cabinets, and a stack of folding chairs.

I stood there like an idiot until Harmony emerged from the back room and introduced herself. She was a short, stocky Black woman who laughed while shaking my hand; I wasn't sure why she was laughing. I wondered if it was something about me, like my fly was open. I resisted the urge to check. She immediately started teasing. Stuff like "You must be the wright man for the job, yeah?" She guffawed at everything and rolled her body with restless vigor. I wasn't sure what to think, having never been interviewed for a job, let alone by a bawdy, irreverent Black woman. I had little to no experience interacting with Black people and assumed there must be some kind of secret to it. I hesitated in my responses, trying to calibrate sensible phrases; mostly I settled for a vacant smile. I figured that Harmony was a lesbian because she looked like several women I'd met who called themselves "dykes." She didn't just fit this look, she flaunted it: plaid work shirt, jeans, leather boots, watch cap pulled tight over short hair, and a dangerous swagger. I was completely outside my comfort zone. I'm sure she knew it and made the most of the opportunity. And yet, as we sat facing each other for the interview, she grinned and slapped my knees and overwhelmed me with her glee. I didn't know how to respond, but I chuckled like I did, just to cover my anxiety. Right away, I understood there would be a learning curve. But her energy filled me to the brim; how could I not like her? In between all the fooling around, she asked the right questions, the questions I'd want to know about a fellow worker. I couldn't read her at all, though, and garnered no idea what she thought of me.

Walking out the front door in a daze, I wondered what the hell I'd done. Having severed my connection to the familiar, no matter how tired of it I was, I now faced the vertigo of the unknown. Harmony said they'd talk over my application in committee and get back to me. To be rejected at this point would have been devastating; despite the anxiety, I'd already made the emotional leap. The Marmot group represented something outside of my experience, but I wanted to be a part of it. Whatever drew me on, the collective seemed to offer more than just another tree planting job.

I went back to our cabin in the North Cascades and waited, trying not to bicker with Debby about stupid things. I fretted over the impression I might have made in the interview, another unsophisticated White male. I doubted my qualifications for being a social revolutionary. Of course, I did have tree planting experience. That probably counted for something. A couple of weeks later I picked up a letter at the post office box. Marmot wanted me to join them on a trial basis in Chelan, where they were planting trees on a Forest Service contract.

I drove my 58 Chevy pickup with Debby and Sam, our three-year-old son, filling out the front seat. Deb would leave me at the camp and drive the truck home. Somehow, I'd get back after the job, probably by hitch-hiking. Bouncing along gravel roads from the shore of Lake Chelan toward the Marmot camp in the hills, we transitioned out of barren, arid lowlands to majestic parks of Ponderosa Pine. After a long ascent, we found the Marmot camp. I got out, dumped my gear on the ground and said goodbye. It was a brief farewell; the way things had been going with our relationship, we both knew it was more than a routine parting.

I took a breath and let it go, feeling the separation. We'd been together for seven years, but it was over. Even though I felt vulnerable, I was ready for whatever came next. Looking around at the Marmot camp, I thought it could have been an advertisement for nomadic competence. Settled on a grassy sward between a grove of pines and the shore of a small lake, it resembled the orderly, idyllic spreads in travel magazines. I counted four canvas tents with protruding stovepipes, a pickup camper, a small trailer, and an old flatbed truck with a cedar-shingled cabin on the back. At the hub of the camp stood a huge white yurt, a modern adaptation of Mongolian technology. On the far side of the yurt, in the grass near the edge of the lake was a low canvas dome with a fire pit in front. Of course, there would be a sweat lodge. And parked on the shore were two slender kayaks, invitations to explore the mirror surface of the lake. I was impressed. We'd never imagined half of this stuff in Gus' crew.

It was a quiet camp, with no one in sight. I walked to the yurt and opened the plywood door. The ceiling caught my attention: a broad cone supported by a couple dozen poles. The butts rested on the circular wall of wooden lattice, the peak ends slotted into a wooden ring, and the whole was covered by a fitted circle of canvas. I liked the bright interior and the sensation of space. Along the far wall a counter had been set up next to a propane cookstove. A man stood over the counter chopping vegetables. I only saw his back and a long, golden-hued ponytail. "Hello?"

He turned and smiled through a wispy beard. "Hi! Are you James? I'm Paul."

I agreed that I was James. "Where is everybody?"

Paul answered that the crew was in the hills working on a unit. He was cook and camp tender for the day. He explained that camp duties were rotated through the whole crew, with each member expected to take his or her turn when the time came. A camp tender did whatever was necessary to keep the crew working. If firewood was needed, you chopped firewood. Camp was cleaned, stores sorted, lists made, all the work that'd been left to the female auxiliary in the Swinging Hoedads.

"How many are on this crew?" I asked.

"You make sixteen," he said.

"I've never cooked for that many people." Here was something else to worry about.

"You'll be okay. Just make soup. Some people are good cooks and get into elaborate stuff, but most just do the best they can. If you screw up, you might get some free advice, that's all." Paul put me at ease with his manner. He was a tall, broad-shouldered man with a soft demeanor. I'd say it was feminine except that it wasn't, not really, just different from the tough, bantering exterior I usually associated with men. Paul gave me a tour of the food supplies, stacked in boxes and coolers under the counter and along the wall. I saw an entire crate full of avocados. I'd never eaten one and couldn't imagine why they were there. "Massive protein," according to Paul. Cardboard boxes held carrots, potatoes, onions, garlic, rice, pasta, and other staples. Bread, of course, and the ubiquitous peanut butter. Finally, he showed me a large flat box filled with a layer of dirt, out of which grew a carpet of thin grass. "Wheatgrass," he announced with pride. What the fuck was wheatgrass, I wondered? I didn't say that, of course, merely raised an eyebrow. "More protein," Paul said, "not to mention mega vitamins and minerals."

"Meat?" I asked.

"We only do vegetarian meals. Some people eat meat, but they have to bring it and cook it on their own. It's bad for you, anyway." Paul would have been a good argument for that assertion: he radiated health. I was certain he'd never committed a bad deed in his life, and I wondered if there really was a place for me amidst such ethereal folk.

Paul said the crew wouldn't be back until dusk and then I'd want to talk to Becky and Dave, who were the coordinators for the contract. Meanwhile, I could set up a shelter wherever I wanted and relax for now. I could even take one of the kayaks out for a spin.

Humbled, I walked into the trees and found a spot for my tent. I picked a flat area, heavy with pine needles, a little farther away from the yurt than everyone else. It didn't take long to set up; I could have done it in my sleep. Like every other tent I'd owned, it was a two-person mountain tent, lightweight and compact for backpacking and sturdy enough to endure all sorts of weather. After tucking my gear inside, I sat down with my back against a wide pine trunk and surveyed the compound. My blue and yellow tent looked like the smallest shelter in camp, a cocoon in comparison to the canvas wall tents down by the lake. I didn't mind, I always slept in something like this when I worked in the woods or roamed the backcountry. It was worth it for the portability; the whole thing packed into a bag the size of a large loaf of bread. By that point, I calculated that I'd spent almost three calendar years of my life sleeping in mountain tents, including sitting out ferocious mountain storms for days on end. Here, in Chelan's dry climate, I anticipated no more than crawling in to sleep and crawling out when the sun came up. If I needed more shelter than that, the yurt seemed downright congenial.

The shadows of late afternoon stretched through the woods by the time the workers returned. One after another, three bright red crew cabs pulled to a stop in the gravel. Of course, the trucks were red, how could they be any other color? Doors slammed and I heard a swirl of voices, female and male, a familiar chorus of tired bodies ready for food. I sauntered down to the yurt and endured the embarrassment of introducing myself to strangers. I sat on a folding chair, spooning in Paul's hearty soup while trying to meet with Becky. She started to tell me a few things, but kept getting distracted by people coming and going, dealing with the details of the job. The conversations went by in a blur and reminded me why I don't go to parties. Dave was up at his trailer, Becky said, and I should go introduce myself.

I left the bustle of the yurt and noticed several naked women crawling into the sweat lodge. On the other side of the compound, two scruffy men sat outside Dave's shelter, a dented trailer with missing chrome strips and no pretension to style. They grilled meat over a barbecue while listening to AC/DC blaring from a tape deck. When I got closer, I heard sarcastic banter and I thought I might be back in the land of the Swinging Hoedads. When I introduced myself, Dave crushed my hand. "We need experienced planters," he said. "Glad to have you aboard." Then he flashed a grin so devilish, I thought I might have sold my soul.

I said I was glad to be there, but I wasn't entirely sure about that. After exchanging a few quips, I continued into the woods and crawled in my tent. As I lay in my sleeping bag, staring into the darkness, I heard women's voices down by the lake, chanting something mysterious and spiritual. Meanwhile, Dave was now listening to Black Sabbath. I imagined the meat juice dripping down his bearded chin. Despite these distractions, I was tired and had no trouble easing into slumber. While consciousness waned, I wondered if this is what it felt like to run away and join the circus.

12

Under the Volcano

My first day planting alongside the Marmots passed with ease. I didn't have to worry about devising maneuvers or figuring out the topographic secrets of the unit, I just followed along and did the same as everyone else. They didn't march in line formation across the clearcut, thank god, but folks weren't spread out into personal enclaves, either. Sort of a mix. Marmots planted at their own pace and if someone was going faster, they hopped over and switched lines, no harm done. I didn't catch a whiff of competition. People strived for planting quality, and I had no problem with that. I bent to the labor and did my thing; it was second nature. As far as I could tell, nobody even counted their trees. Everybody got paid eight dollars an hour. If you worked for the collective for a couple of years, you got a raise. There were no eleven-hour days, the pace was reasonable, and the food was good if you didn't mind an abundance of vegetables. I heard few complaints and dispositions seemed bright, perhaps even enthusiastic. If we had straw hats and ribbons, you'd think we were working on the farm at Green Gables.

By the middle of May we neared the end of the Chelan contract. I'd been hired on a trial basis, but I could tell they were happy with my production. And I was happy with them. Whatever loyalties lingered from my old associations, they'd been erased. I even survived my duty as camp cook, or at least no one complained within my hearing. I decided that I wanted to be a full-fledged member of the collective.

During the month at Chelan, I developed crushes on some of the women, but settled for admiring them from a distance. I had a hard time figuring out who was with who, or if people paired up, stayed fluid, or what. It seemed prudent to simply watch and learn. The ambiance of the crew floated plenty of libido, though, and it was contagious. I opted to channel this energy into writing poetry. Some of these poems seemed urgent enough to post on the walls of the yurt, sharing my overwrought lyrics with the collective. The poems weren't good, but there they were, and some people claimed to like them. Many said nothing. No one was rude, so I continued this practice until I got tired of wallowing in the vapors.

Throughout the spring we followed the news reports about seismic disturbances beneath Mount St. Helens. Everybody in Washington had an opinion about the volcano, how interesting it was, what are the chances, who cares, and the occasional apocalyptic fantasy, all loaded with idle speculation and detached concern. Even though there are five volcanoes in the state, there had been no major eruptions since white folks took up residence, white folks who don't think much about geological time scales. So what if scientists predicted that St. Helens would erupt? No one knew what that meant, exactly, which led to believing that nothing much would happen.

On May 18, we drove to the top of a clear-cut ridge to plant the last unit of the contract. The views were exceptional, overlooking the foothills along the eastern side of the Cascades all the way to the high peaks in the west. We expected to finish before the end of the day, at which point we'd pack camp and the Marmots would head back to Seattle. I'd already decided to go with them. Even though it was the last tree planting contract of the season, I hoped to find a place on one of their summer jobs, maybe trail construction. I didn't want to part from the group and its anarchist energy just to resume my old life. If I could avoid a little longer the pain of disentangling the threads of my foundering relationship, that's what I would do.

The crew spread across the unit, and we covered the ground in good style. With the end in sight, we planted faster than usual, eager for the last tree and the satisfaction of completion. We'd been working for an hour when I heard a series of distant explosions. I stopped planting and gazed to the south. It sounded like thunder, but continuous, like a repeating cannon: BOOM BOOM BOOM BOOM. Without a break, it went on for a long time, paused, then started again. After several more minutes of rumbling, silence returned. I'd never heard anything like it. I don't know why, but I didn't think of Mt. St. Helens. If a volcano blew and you were near enough to hear it, I figured it'd be one memorable KA-BOOM followed by oblivion. Instead, and I suppose this reveals my state of the mind at the time, I thought it was the Chinese. The headlines had claimed they now had an atomic bomb and intercontinental missiles capable of delivering the package. The situation produced an intense political tension between the US and China and a lot of people experienced a re-emergence of their 50s childhood memories accompanied by old atomic anxieties. I grew up doing weekly drills in elementary school, curled under my desk waiting for the all-clear signal. So, naturally, I figured we were being attacked. We shouted at each other back and forth across the unit: "What the hell is that?" "I dunno, maybe it's the Chinese!" "The Chinese?!" "Sure, why not?" "Shit, not the Chinese!"

Since we had no way to confirm these speculations, we did what all dedicated workers do, which is continue the work. On the southern horizon, a dense haze rose into the sky. We watched as we planted in haste, responding to an urgency to finish. In an hour or so, a Forest Service pickup came speeding up the road to the unit, braked to a halt in a cloud of dust, and the driver yelled for attention. Somebody went down to check on the fuss. The word came back along the line: St. Helens had erupted. The top of the mountain was gone, and the nearest town had been rubbed off the map. According to the Forest Service, an ash cloud of cataclysmic proportions was headed our way. They advised us to shut down operations and flee the area immediately. They ended with a legal admonishment to "consider that you have been dutifully warned and your official representative is now leaving." After announcing the release of liability, the Forest Service worker roared off down the road. Apparently, it was up to us to sort out the coming of Armageddon.

With eerie silence, the sky to the south grew darker as ash obscured the sun. Mt. St. Helens was about 150 air miles away. The ash cloud was reported to be moving very quickly but after worrying that we would be engulfed in minutes, there was no obvious advance. It just seemed to rise higher above the mountain. Or where the mountain had been. We studied the unit we needed to finish and figured that we had maybe an hour or two of work left. "Let's do it," we all agreed, and planted like little demons so we could skedaddle to safety as recommended by the government of the United States of America.

We completed the unit, drove back to camp, and immediately convened a meeting in the yurt. We had two choices: pack up right away and make a dash for Seattle or hunker down and wait for doom. The sky was ominous, but it hadn't started raining ash, frogs, blood, or any other notable signs of the end of the world. We were all outside our zones of experience, so we argued. A large contingent wanted to get the hell out of there. The other contingent wanted to sit tight and stay put—we had food, shelter, water, and everything we needed to survive for a week or so. Both courses of action were based on the same fact: we didn't have any idea how this was going to play out. Rumors of paralyzing ash rains and other biblical-type spectacles remained rumors. Our information came from the radio, and that seemed more confusing than useful. How to decide? I supported the stay-put contingent. Having already outlived direct attack from the Chinese, I found my science fiction-trained imagination fully engaged with the idea of a post-apocalypse scenario. We were in a lovely sanctuary, we had what we needed, we could rebuild society! We tried to make a sober assessment of the situation, but it was crazy, no one knew what to do, and, in the end, we stayed put.

It turned out that the flee-in-panic crowd was correct; we should have left. We could have made it back to Seattle before nightfall, dodging the ash cloud, which never passed over Puget Sound. Instead, it went north and east, dumping enormous amounts of ash on eastern Washington. Towns like Yakima were paralyzed under a foot of the toxic fluff, using snowplows to move it off the streets. But ash is not snow—it can destroy an internal combustion engine within hours. Without specialized air filters, the razor-sharp particles get into the pistons, scoring the cylinder walls, resulting in almost complete loss of compression. If you can get the engine to run, it has no power. And breathing ash is a serious health hazard—the fragments can slice your lungs as fast as inhaling a weed whacker, as I'd already learned in Northern Idaho. Volcanic ash is particularly nasty stuff. The thought of it falling from the sky in a deluge, erasing the sun, left us to imagine a disaster of mythic proportions.

Ash descended on our Chelan camp all through the night, but not much, an inch or less. Then it was over. We milled around in the morning, trying to take stock of what catastrophe would happen next. Nothing, it seemed. So, we swept the gray powder off our possessions and drove to Seattle, abandoning my utopian fantasies to the dust.

13

MARMCO

During the summer, Marmot worked on trail construction contracts in National Parks or Wilderness Areas. To me, that sounded like a dream come true. I imagined it as a labor of love in my favorite landscapes; between refreshing pauses to absorb the vistas, we'd build rock paths, stone steps, retaining walls, and all sorts of cool zen things. As an added attraction, you got to blow up stuff with dynamite. The fact that I had originally approached tree planting with a similar gloss of glamorous unreality hardly dissuaded me from trail building fantasies. I'd spent years walking all over the North Cascades on mountain paths; no activity pleased me more. Despite that, I never thought about the work of creating them. That you could call it a job and get paid seemed outlandish. I had to do it. Unfortunately, everyone thought the same. There were only limited slots available for the summer of 80, and being a newbie, I didn't get picked. If I had a blaster's license, I could have vaulted into a position. But the idea of getting a license to explode rocks was another thing that had never crossed my mind. Then, as soon as the current job ended,

Marmot stopped bidding on trails. Those contracts tended to lose money and the labor turned out to be brutal and unenlightening. Workers reported feeling more like slaves than buddhas, so I crossed it off my bucket list.

Without a trail job, I drifted back to my mountain cabin, disappointed and confused about how I should transition into collective life. But it was only a collective for workers; when you weren't working, you were on your own. Some members shared housing, but I didn't feel that I knew anyone well enough to worm a way into their homes. So, I returned to the cabin and the eroded remains of my family.

Halfway through the summer, I traveled to Bellingham to attend the collective's general meeting, held once a year. For two days everyone assembled to hear reports from committees and make decisions. We heard from a bidding committee, a finance committee, a vehicle committee, and a tool committee. Each group consisted of three or four members who were empowered to make operational decisions. When they brought their concerns to the general meeting, they sought endorsement through a consensus of the full assembly. If consensus couldn't be achieved with explanations and debate, decisions were left to majority rule. And that's how we governed ourselves. We agreed on many things, but ended up voting often, because consensus was never simple. There's always someone with a different perspective and few groups can survive bending everyone into consensus. Sometimes, you just need to move on whether everyone agrees or not.

Collective governance requires participation. As a result, we had all sorts of meetings. There were meetings on the job at base camp, there were meetings back in the city, no matter where we were, we had meetings. Most people can't tolerate that, which may be the fatal flaw in democratic anarchism. We complained about the endless meetings but still took it seriously. To facilitate this format, Marmot provided training in productive participation. Sort of a *Robert's Rules of Order* for revolutionaries. At first, I was skeptical of the structure, but in all the years of meetings I attended since Marmot, I've never seen them handled more efficiently or where so many people understood their roles. Human behavior in meeting situations often generates a subversive element, where participants like to polarize against the boss or facilitator or whoever is trying to run the meeting. Whether the behavior is jokey, withdrawn, or contentious, few folks in the hierarchical world seem to grasp the importance of working together in group process. Marmot meetings were a revelation to me, and although they weren't always smooth or as brief as one might like—try sitting through a two-hour meeting in the evening after a full day of tree planting—there was a commitment to making the process achieve its goals. This is the price to be paid if you don't want a boss.

During the two days of the general meeting, I met the rest of the Marmots, the ones who weren't at the Chelan job. Some had taken time off while the remainder had worked another contract. Marmot often fielded two crews, especially at the height of tree planting season. Once you became a member, you got paid when you worked, but there didn't seem to be a minimum requirement. People drifted in and out of the fold with a casual air, sometimes working with other cooperative crews through the open doors of the NWFWA network. That left Marmot's business in the hands of committed regulars. Being a loyalist, I couldn't understand the floating around. I wanted to be in the core, a true Marmot.

At the general meeting, I watched how the collective worked as an organization. I didn't know enough to have opinions, and I still felt shy around the bustle of the group, so I kept my mouth shut and observed. Most of the matters were boring, especially the bureaucratic details. I recognized the necessity to deal with these details, but that didn't make them compelling. However, one issue at the general meeting catalyzed the proceedings. By any sane measure, it was trivial, yet it grabbed me by the ankle and wouldn't let go. The legal name of the collective had always been Marmot Construction Works, Ltd. Some folks opined that this name was confusing for a reforestation company that did no construction outside of occasional trail work. I had wondered about that myself. A few core members wanted to change it to something more streamlined and suitable for public consumption, especially since everyone knew us as just plain "Marmot."

The assembly of two-dozen women and men, excited to have an amusing diversion, quickly generated a long list of names. Most of these involved permutations around the word "marmot." That was one of the things that drew me to the collective in the first place. A marmot is a chunky sub-alpine rodent resembling its lower-elevation cousin the woodchuck. I was infatuated with them. There was the obvious roly-poly factor: they were shy and adorable. When walking summer trails into the high meadows of the North Cascades, one of the first things you hear are the clear whistles of marmots, warning each other about your approach. Despite these collective alarms, if you sit quietly in the meadow, the marmots eventually come out and waddle around, munching on flowers and checking you out from a safe distance. I have a treasured photo of a marmot sniffing at the handle of my ice axe as it was stuck in the ground about twenty feet from where I sat. In the background, rock summits and hanging glaciers provide the context. My memories of rambling in steep terrain merged marmots and mountains into a joyful emblem. Of course, I wanted to work under this name, as if the mammal itself was my employer.

It's an old problem of mine, this irrational identification with things as symbols. If I found a deer antler laying in the woods, I tended to look for the cosmic message, like it had been left for me. If I saw a film about the masses of humankind overthrowing their oppressors, I cried as if my own downtrodden soul had, at long last, been liberated from the grip of fascism. In those days of personal turbulence I would have preferred to be a marmot, snug in a furry pelt, gazing across a pristine alpine meadow onto the sullied world below.

There was a contingent at the general meeting that wanted to do away with the word "marmot." Too soft and fuzzy, they said—to me, an unfathomable criticism. They thought more professional nomenclature would improve our image. Objections were raised and polarization developed between the hard-boiled revolutionaries who were unattached to bourgeois trivialities like names and the feel-good rebels who flew the banner of warm fuzziness with pride. Some odd compromises emerged, such as the contraction "Marmco." For a while I was afraid that would be the new name.

Even though I had virtually no history with the group, I got carried away with my own sentimentality. I gave up the bystander role and passionately argued for retention of the word "marmot," proclaiming that the glory of the word should be plenty. I got caught up in my own rhetoric, and threatened to resign if marmot was not in the name, never mind that I had just been voted into full membership the day before. This, of course, set me up for some well-deserved sarcasm and more than a few funny looks. In retrospect, my conduct was embarrassing, as was often the case. Yet no one could appreciate how far I had gone down the road of becoming an industrial tree planting machine before coming to Marmot. I had worn that reality and tried to make it my own. But I was done with it. Now I wanted a soft fur coat and snuggly comrades. That's just where I was at.

Despite my outbursts and after much lively debate, the collective settled on the name "Marmot, Inc.," pronounced "marmot ink". Fuzziness intact, we closed the general meeting, and I walked away, comfortable in my fur.

14

Under the Volcano Redux

If you live and work in the woods, at some point you'll think about getting a chainsaw. Lester and Peter and other Swinging Hoedads had talked about those noisy, stinky devices in terms that glowed with the male fondness for machines. I listened to their raptures and eventually owned three saws, counting the old, broken McCulloch stuffed in the shed. The McCulloch was my first, an obsolete, cheap acquisition that I soon regretted. Heavy and cranky, I couldn't keep it running and it cut slower than a handsaw. It hardly sold me on power wood cutting. I'd sweated over old-timey crosscut saws, though, and had no desire to go back to the blisters and backaches. Surely, there was potential with internal combustion. Following Lester's recommendation, I finally purchased a brand-new German-made Stihl 040. It sliced through firewood like butter, shaped the logs that went into the cabins I built, and cut down trees and brush for all the reasons a forest dweller can muster for cutting trees and brush. With that saw, more than with any car I owned, I fell in love with fossil fuel consumption.

As my ambitions grew for sawing wood, I purchased a monster, the Stihl 075, the biggest chainsaw I could find. It featured a seven-horsepower engine and a three-foot bar. Very few of my friends could even start this saw. I smirked and watched them try. It wasn't just about strength, you had to know the saw, how to pull the cord with the correct enthusiasm and confidence. A casual yank brought the pretender to his knees in surprise. The 075 was not to be toyed with; it was a fucking beast. I used it for falling big trees and milling slabs of wood, including the two-foot-wide pine boards that became the floor of my first cabin. I avoided power tools in general, but I loved my chainsaws for the fierce industry of their work. And a sharp, well-tuned saw can work all day, sucking through tank after tank of carbon-spewing gasoline.

My skills as a sawyer came in handy with Marmot. A cohort within the collective was keen on timber thinning contracts, technically a subset of the overall reforestation endeavor, but requiring its own set of specialty tools and know-how. Because thinning contracts run in summer and fall, they offer an extension of the spring planting season. I'd cut down trees before, but I'd never worked on a timber thinning job, so I was curious. Many Marmots found chainsaw work distasteful and refused to do it. Not me; other guys got off on motorcycles, but for me it was chainsaws. After the general meeting, I eagerly packed my gear and joined the crew dedicated to weeding trees rather than planting them.

In the fall of 1980, Marmot had a large precommercial thinning contract in the Naches Ranger District, just east of Mount Rainier and approximately seventy miles north of what was left of Mount St. Helens. That's the official name for the job: precommercial thinning. Because bureaucrats can't get enough abbreviations, it's usually referred to as PCT. The name reveals the subtext of forest management: precommercial because the crop is thinned before it reaches maturity for commercial logging. The acronym jams the show into a management box. It's not a forest; it's a crop and the things we do to it are always in code.

The Naches contract was a big one, so the Marmot tool committee purchased twenty brand-new Husqvarna chainsaws for the job. I preferred the Stihl brand, but the Swedish Husqvarna was the lightest and quietest on the market. A major investment for the collective, we aimed to move further into the PCT game. The Husky chainsaws would be a strong asset in taking on more contracts. Shelling out ten or twenty grand was a hit, but I admired the collective willingness to go for it.

All the tools we used had to be maintained and replaced; our productivity derived from the material means of production. The tool committee had its hands full staying on top of enough stuff to fill a warehouse. Marmot's inventory included three new Ford crew cab pickups, an enormous GMC two-ton truck with a bus-like personnel carrier mounted on the back, three twenty-foot yurts, ten canvas wall tents, lightweight wood stoves, propane cookstoves, and hundreds of hand items like shovels, hoedads, pulaskis, axes, hammers, knives, kitchenware, and more. Pretty much everything we handled on the job was a tool. The tool committee not only kept us working, it also offered an outlet for the geeks.

The Naches job was in progress by the time I arrived at camp. Straight away, I ran into Steve, Marmot's hard-core Communist, who greeted me like a brother because he'd heard that I liked working with saws. Steve loved chainsaws with a proletarian ardor. I'd first met him at the general meeting where I learned that he avoided tree planting because it bored him. I continued to hear stories about Steve, and he populated my imagination as a legend. The basic idea was that he "had a lot of energy," although the alternate version was that he was "a little crazy." Steve's parents had been members of the Communist Party and he had grown up in an atmosphere of revolutionary rhetoric. Rumors claimed that he carried an assault rifle in his vehicle because he didn't want to be caught off guard when the revolution started.

Steve owned a giant Cuban flag, about six feet by eight feet. He liked to hang it on the side of the yurt just in case anyone was unclear about our affinities. If the collective voted on this display it happened before my time, or maybe it never happened at all because a wide spectrum of free expression was tolerated, even encouraged. That anarchist thing. Besides, the flag provided a recurring source of amusement when government officials visited the camp. You could rely on the inevitable double take when a Forest Service representative recognized the flag, and then the fidgeting began. The flag was so large that you couldn't go anywhere in camp without it being in your face. Worth displaying, if only to pretend that it didn't exist while the lackeys of the state squirmed in discomfort.

We had a big crew at Naches, but there was a problem with the job. It had been four months since the eruption of Mt. St. Helens. During the May cataclysm, most of the ash had blown north and east from the mountain and had dumped plenty on Naches. Subsequent eruptions, smaller in scope, had occurred since May, resulting in more ash drifting north of the volcano. By September, it seemed that the mountain was settling back into dormancy, but the ash that had rained into the woods hadn't gone away. The thinning units were ten-year-old planting sites that had grown into dense jungles of natural reproduction among the planted trees. The regrowth was vigorous, ten to twenty feet tall, and packed tight. Heavy with foliage, every horizontal surface, every leaf and needle in the forest, was now cloaked in layers of ghostly gray ash.

Timber thinning works like any other crop thinning. You designate the best trees as leave trees, then cut everything else down, like you might weed and thin your garden. Instead of kneeling in your carrot patch and carefully sorting through the dirt with your fingers, timber thinning involves samurai maneuvers. The worker's costume embodies the role: helmet with face shield or separate goggles, heavy padded chaps on your legs to absorb the blows when you accidentally bounce the spinning saw blade against your leg, thick gloves, caulk boots for sure-footed balance while wading through the stems and branches, and any other pieces of armor you might care to add to increase your chances of emerging unscathed from combat. It took me a while to adjust to wearing so much protective clothing for intense labor; it was uncomfortable and left you feeling like a hockey player without a rink. But the timber thinner lives in a world of spinning saw blades and falling trees. Protection is a good thing. I soon discovered that the primary threat was inattention, like always, which could lead to a saw bouncing back out of a cluster of stems. That didn't have to happen too many times before you learned to stay focused. A rogue chainsaw was not your friend.

The most efficient body movements to weed trees could best be described as "mowing." Imagine the motion of using a scythe to harvest grain, only replace the scythe with a chainsaw running at full throttle. The thinner sweeps the saw back and forth in front of him or herself, slicing through the wrist-sized stems, mowing down the outcasts. As the stems fall to the left, right, and on one's head, the thinner shrugs them off with elbows, shoulders, and helmet, bulldozing forward into the thickets of young trees, selecting survivors in the grace of an instant, then slaughtering the rest. A savage task, and a perfect conduit for repressed anger. Indeed, the rush of power that came with the job went straight to my head. Absolute, pure, contained destruction—and I got paid to do it.

Everything I learned about how to do this job I learned from watching Steve the Commie and Toshiro Mifune movies. Nobody could keep up with Steve's sword of revolutionary zeal; he was possessed. Whenever I could, I worked next to him, not only because he was efficient, safe, and always ready to help a comrade in need, but because I loved watching him work. His communion with the energy of destruction achieved complete balance, a manifestation of Kali set free in the woods, a merger of grace and fury. Be like Steve, I told myself, be like him and you will not only live through this experience, you might even enjoy it.

To understand the situation facing us at Naches, consider the respiratory consequences of mowing through thickets of dusty trees. As you slice the stems, the cut trees fall left and right, sliding off your head and shoulders on their descent, and every square inch of every branch is covered with dry volcanic ash. It reminded me of the ash clouds we'd kicked up scalping the ground on the burning Idaho unit I'd planted with Swinging Hoedads. Only this was much worse. The ash at Naches formed a personal cloud from which you didn't emerge until you turned off the saw and backed out of it. Filter masks for breathing became essential armor. Unfortunately, we didn't fully understand that the machines needed to breathe, too. The ash clogged the air filters on the saws, shutting the saw down and choking the life out of it. We carried spare filters, cleaned filters in the field, did everything we could, but it was a challenge to keep your saw running through the day. And if you did, a few days later you'd discover that despite all these precautions, the ash still managed to penetrate the cylinders, scoring the pistons and walls until there was no compression left. The saws—including the lovely new Husqvarnas—soon had no power and couldn't do the work.

Our evenings were filled with hours of maintenance work, not much fun after a hard day. Many saws needed to have cylinders and pistons replaced on a regular basis. The tool committee experts were trying to develop new technologies to meet the crisis. They installed large exterior air filters on the saws to create additional zones of protection for the machines. None of their interventions really worked, nor did the use of a face mask prevent one from inhaling ash. We developed chronic coughs, just like the Swinging Hoedads in Idaho. There is something terrifying about coughing up globs of black phlegm every morning when you roll out of bed. We talked of nothing else and collectively veered towards panic. It was a hellish job and would kill us in the end, sputtering and hacking like our saws as we coughed ourselves into the final rest. We had escaped major volcanic consequences during the initial eruption; was it now going to carve its mark into our lungs?

So, we did what we had to do: we quit. After discussions and meetings, we packed up camp and left the job. When we got back to Seattle, we filed a claim against the government that the contract environment did not provide reasonable working conditions. True enough. After a winter or two of snow and rain, most of the ash would be rinsed off the trees. The contract should have been postponed. Of course, no one had anticipated the potential impact of a volcanic eruption; it's fair to say that the circumstances were unpredictable. Once our problems had been presented to the Forest Service, though, they could have cancelled the job and postponed it or put it up for bid later. Instead, they turned around and filed a claim against Marmot for breach of contract. When this matter finally arrived in court, years later, the judge offset the claims against each other, deciding that Marmot did leave the job early and therefore wouldn't be reimbursed for additional expenses, but also decreed that the conditions on the job were unacceptable and therefore no penalty was levied for breaching the contract.

Naches did nothing to expand the popularity of thinning within the collective. But there were a few of us, besides Steve, who liked it well enough. The pace was different; we worked shorter days for safety reasons, never more than five or six hours. And unlike tree planting, instead of wading through brush and slash to find new homes for seedlings, you swept away the congested greenery, leaving a widely spaced park of young trees. The results often looked tidy and agricultural. Noise, sharp steel, and the combustion of gasoline combined to alter the very shape of the forest. Who now was master of the woods? There was a mythic quality to this hubris, an emotional justification that allowed you to feel ennobled by the act of striding across the landscape killing flora. Never mind the rational arguments about how we needed lumber and paper and all that, and even how thinning was an important step in the reforestation process, freeing up the trees to grow faster, none of that influenced me as much as the irrational glamor of sculpting the forest. As much pride as I accumulated over time from planting trees, I also loved the rush of cutting them down.

Thinning was fun, at least for a while. Then I started to notice the early symptoms of Raynaud's Syndrome, a neurological condition that can lead to permanent numbness in the extremities. Caused by persistent vibration and cold, the condition developed from compromised circulation. Thinning, though hard work, was a more stationary job than tree planting. Hands and feet were often chilled and did not get the constant pumping of blood involved in hiking rapidly back and forth across the unit. We ran our saws at high rpms, soaking up the tingles in our arms. Steve, always full of practical advice, showed me a useful trick: when your hands got too cold, you could put your saw on the ground, take off your glove and hold the open cuff over the exhaust port of the idling saw. The saw blew hot exhaust straight into the glove, making it toasty warm. I thought this was nifty and used it often, although always with the suspicion that I was absorbing exhaust fumes through my skin. Probably that's impossible, but I was obsessed about it. Then, I'd pull off my gloves to stare at the ashy, white color of my fingers. They looked like the hands of Death, so I'd stick the gloves back on the exhaust. You couldn't dwell on the future, not in this line of work.

15

A Field Guide to Marmots

Now that I was a full-fledged Marmot, my labor would be part of a collective system bringing the socialist future into the present. Or so I imagined. Heady stuff for a former boy communist. Having worked on two contracts, I saw how it was with the job, and now I wanted to learn how things worked behind the scenes. Who was with whom and how did I fit in? As someone in retreat from a long-term relationship, with loneliness on the horizon, I looked at the women in Marmot with interest. There was a dearth of obvious relationships, at least as far as I could tell, amidst a liberal sexual ambiance. Amorous possibilities seemed to float as freely as pheromones. There were no kids in Marmot and very few couples. In fact, couples were considered by many to be a manifestation of regressive bourgeois practices. Most people seemed to endorse the old anarchist creed of "free love," agreeing with Emma Goldman, who said, "As if love is anything but free!" Second wave feminism was ascendant in American society, homosexuals were edging out of the closet, and you didn't have to be an anarchist to get caught up in the dynamics of open relationships, sexual identity, and the allure of variety.

Despite the revolutionary passion, the daily comportment of the collective didn't strike me as unusually wanton. Sometimes you could see women flirting and kissing with each other and acting like straight couples do in public. But I didn't stumble into orgies in the yurt or anything like that. And I never saw porn in the crummy. Feminism was the paradigm, not Playboy.

Some of the Marmot men were gay or bisexual but most of them didn't advertise it. Underlying passions occasionally percolated to the surface, though. One fellow, whose gender affiliations I never did understand, I encountered on the porch of a Seattle house where a Marmot party was being held. As we stood on the steps and waited for someone to answer the door, he pulled a massive dildo out of a bag and thrust it in my face, waving and wiggling it lewdly. I couldn't decode his muttering, whether I was being propositioned or spoofed—he was too drunk to take seriously either way. Inside the party, he accosted one person after another with the plastic dong and raved obscenities. Clearly, he had a message. I assumed that he was horny, but for whom or what was hard to pin down. Maybe it didn't matter.

Unlike the women, I never saw men kissing or petting. A little discrete hand holding was all. The most openly gay man in the collective often engaged in saucy or flirtatious talk, perhaps just to keep everybody loose and grounded in his reality. Once, he planted trees in a tutu. He planted a lot of trees and looked cute doing it. Then, it was back to jeans and work shirts.

It was the straights and their behaviors that tended to rock the collective equanimity. When I arrived at the Chelan job, gossip had been circulating about a guy who was in a relationship with one Marmot woman but had started sleeping with another woman in the collective; now there were problems with who could and couldn't work together. The women were assigned to different contracts to keep the peace, an expedient response if not a solution. The scandal floated in and out of crew conversations and everyone seemed to have a strong opinion. I heard the talk although I'd just walked onto the job and didn't know any of the parties. I listened with detached amusement; glad they weren't talking about me. Having emerged from my own melodrama, I found it reassuring that even the radicals of the new society weren't immune to human shortcomings.

Despite the odd excitement, the collective behaviors were unsurprising for a cluster of mostly unattached twenty- and thirty-year-olds working and living together. I don't know what I expected; free love means different things to different people. Yet it wasn't Sunday school, either. I remember one cold, windy day of tree planting, when I walked off the unit to the crummy to get more trees and get out of the weather. Shortly after crawling into the back seat of the crew cab, I was joined by one of the women also taking a break. I had gotten to know her a little and liked her, so we chatted for a bit. We sat next to each other and as I complained about the cold, she picked up one of my hands, slid it up her shirt, and placed it on the skin of her breast. "Warm it up," she said. Speechless, and being slow, I did not respond to what seemed like an unspoken invitation. But was it an invitation? With feminists I was never sure if it was a form of teasing. Combinations of response whirled through my head like the images on a slot machine, resulting in a complete volitional paralysis. I managed a thin smile and quietly warmed my hand as suggested, without exploration. In a few minutes, feeling weird, I withdrew the hand, put it back in my glove, uttered a weak "thank you," and went back to work. She had performed the maneuver with such casual ease that even though I felt like a dolt, awkwardness didn't linger in our relations.

It's liberating to interact with women when you don't feel an obligation to court them. You can laugh and joke, share thoughts, talk nonsense, or vent any feeling, all because you like each other, no strings attached. I can't explain why men are compelled to confirm their desirability with every woman who crosses their paths, some kind of unconscious insecurity, perhaps. No doubt, this is part of the reason why so many women enjoy the company of gay men, which frees them from the objectification of desire.

I enjoyed hanging out with the Marmot lesbians; for one thing, it was pretty clear where you stood with them. They loved to laugh and were a witty, sharp-tongued bunch. It was eye opening to observe women refer to other women as sex objects, often, I think, just to get a reaction from the men who were present. Harmony was merciless in this regard. One time she sauntered up to me and remarked that so-and-so, a new female recruit, "had the hots" for me, all the while she was nudging me, slapping me in the arm and acting the "buddy" part, urging me to make an advance. I wanted to think she was right, but I wasn't sure and suspected she was just pulling my leg. Harmony was often outrageous and made me uncomfortable, which only inspired her to greater efforts. No doubt my hemming, hawing, and emotional discomfort offered her sufficient reward. In retrospect, I'm grateful for these shared moments, these zen teachings from a free woman to the uptight acolyte. Not that I learned much except that I was inhibited, which I already knew.

One of my best friends in Marmot was Jane, a grumpy misfit. She sneered at labels, but if pressed, would proudly call herself a "dyke." Her apparel resembled Harmony's, with the added air of a rumpled, backwoods boy: somber-colored wool shirts, jeans, well-scuffed boots, close-cropped hair, stocking cap pulled tight over her skull. Her acid sarcasm and caustic humor reinforced my own tendencies. I admired her what the hell choices. For example, she smoked cigarettes because they were bad for her. We hit it off right away. Within minutes of meeting, we initiated a running commentary that outlined every absurd feature of whatever was going on, all drenched in merciless black humor. When I introduced Jane to the concept of "heavy air" I didn't have to explain it, she knew exactly what I was talking about, and the recognition of heavy air situations became one of our shared jokes. A true anarchist, she voiced skepticism of Mao, Marx, and the New Age—three pillars of Marmot—all in the same breath. She provided a useful balance for me, correcting my tendencies toward idealistic acceptance of everything Marmot. When it came to emotional experience, I don't remember that we talked too much—my vocabulary for such things was limited, anyway. We developed a comfortable friendship and some things never needed to be said. We were pals if not confidantes. Despite that, years later, when my mother died, I remember Jane being there as a helpful guest, taking care of things around the house, quiet and solid, the kind of companion you need in such times.

As for the men, I knew how to work with men, and it was a relief not to fall into competitive tree counts or the array of macho bullshit that permeated so many work situations. The Marmots, men and women, all worked hard at the job, and I respected that. Outdoing anyone wasn't meaningful, because our energy went toward the collective good and the benefits came back to us. I made more money and collected a regular paycheck instead of a wad of cash at the end of the season. Among the men, I found friends that could talk about cinema, literature, music, politics, and most anything else without embarrassing themselves. And we didn't have to consume prodigious quantities of dope to get the job done. Marijuana was a treat for the end of the day or a special occasion, not the breath of life. It seemed weird, at first, planting sober, but I learned that I didn't need it after all.

Social life in the collective brought a sense of security because we were part of a self-contained community, at least when we were working, and the community took care of us. There were limits to this, but it resembled a tribal band. The presence of the group had given me enough confidence to complete the separation from Debby. It had been my first serious relationship, and I had no idea how to end it. I waffled and wallowed with insecurity. The parting had its intense moments, but we kept the rancor down and maintained a general civility. I needed that.

During the Naches thinning job, I developed a relationship with a strong, open-hearted Marmot woman. Hannah made it clear that she wanted to be with me; I don't know why, but I didn't stop to ask questions. Her big heart was irresistible and I admired her confident independence. The collective, with its commitment to a radical ethos, leaned against exclusive relationships, yet despite that we became a couple that lasted for years. This required a brazen resistance, but we decided that, as anarchists, resistance was our duty.

16

Myrtlewood and Mao

In January, we assembled a large Marmot crew and drove seven hours south for a tree planting contract in the Coast Range of Oregon. It rarely snows within this network of low elevation hills and steep watersheds; you can work the woods year round if you don't mind the persistent rain. Trees grow well in this climate, and the area has been a magnet for the ravenous timber industry. Like loyal mushrooms, tree planters popped up behind the loggers to replenish each new clear-cut. In exchange for a couple hundred years of forest growth, the industry derived a month or two of harvest work, then it was on to the next unit as if there could be no end to it.

With Marmot I was able to work most of the year—a different experience from the seasonal forays of the Swinging Hoedads. Unfortunately, if I wanted to be part of my five-year-old son's life, or pretend to be a parent in any way, I needed to figure out how to incorporate him into my nomadic existence. In the past, his mother provided childcare in tree planting camps, as well as cooking and camp-tending chores shared with the other women allied with Swinging Hoedads. When I'd joined Marmot, I'd left my son with Debby because a man's job had a priority, or so I thought. My new partner, Hannah, saw things differently. She was fond of Sam and wanted to bring him to Oregon. But who would take care of him? I wanted to work and, of course, needed the money.

Hannah outlined the feminist arguments regarding the community obligation toward the care and feeding of children. This, she said, was an essential component of a just society. She pitched this to the rest of the crew during a planning meeting while I nodded along sagely, hesitant to presume that my opinions would add anything of merit. I was surprised when the crew agreed to the proposal of having a child in camp. They quickly decided to establish a pool of volunteer childcare providers who would rotate duties so that I could work. I was surprised and grateful. Even though the collective didn't have a place for kids, most members shared a political interest in developing support systems for raising children, at least on a theoretical level. Of course, theoretical children are a lot easier to manage than real ones, so this endeavor turned into a learning experience for us all. Whether or not the experience would be beneficial to Sam was a question I hadn't thought about asking.

In anticipation of the winter rain, we rented half a dilapidated motel near the wayside town of Myrtle Point. Most of the crew would be able to squeeze into motel rooms, two or three to a cell. Those who wanted privacy, like my own bourgeois family unit, pitched 6' x 10' canvas tents with wood stoves. In the grass next to the motel's moldy playground equipment, we set up one of our big yurts for communal space. The motel let us take over their bathhouse & toilet facility, a nice addition if you weren't too squeamish. The overall effect resembled a carnival squatting in a decayed refuge for lost tourists.

Foot paths between the shelters of our compound turned into sloughs of mud. Given a choice, most people preferred to hang out in the motel rooms; they might smell a little musty, but they were warm and free of leaks. Sam and his caregivers spent most of their days in these rooms, venturing out when the weather relented and scurrying back to shelter when the rains resumed. The caregivers demonstrated a variety of skills. Most of the women could fall back on baby-sitting experience but the men had to learn on the job. In either case, Sam recruited all his caregivers for his endless boy projects. The Marmots who volunteered, and most of them did, were agreeable and obedient playmates, giving Sam constant attention, feeding him freely, and setting no limits. He was an imaginative child and with the assistance of an adult, he played all day, utilizing the complete resources of the camp for endless construction and deconstruction schemes. At the end of the workday, while eating dinner together in the yurt, Hannah and I heard the accounts of these activities narrated by both child and adult as if they were the singular accomplishments of Herakles.

Many professed to enjoy the childcare, while some did it out of duty rather than joy. But they did it. I don't know how we made this happen; in retrospect it seems remarkable. It's humbling to consider all the energy that went into the project, but that was a strength of the collective, a willingness to exercise the muscles of social change. However, this was an experiment we did not repeat. After the job, Sam went back to live with his mother most of the time. The collective still had to compete in a capitalist economy, and labor downtime turned out to be a utopia we couldn't afford.

Out of curiosity about the psychological impact of tree planting camp on an impressionable child, I asked the grownup Sam about his memories of the two months we spent at Myrtle Point in the early 80s. He remembered it as a positive experience, all except for the strange man in the other part of the motel who tried to lure him into his room with the promise of candy. I remember coming back from a day of work to hear about this. My immediate urge was to murder the candy man. My comrades urged restraint since nothing had happened beyond the lure. We all agreed that it was important to keep Sam away from this guy whatever his intentions, so I decided to trust them. Besides, I'd never killed anyone and wasn't even sure how it was done.

Sam, in his memories, emphasized the willingness of his caregivers to assist in the construction of a rock dam in the creek behind the motel. This was a bit of a Sisyphean project and I believe the creek was never diverted from its bed despite the labor, which required the relocation of many rocks. These outings were always followed by "toast attacks," frying the bread on the wood stove in the yurt and scarfing down crisp slices drooling with jam. He also recalled the incessant blaring of the motel loudspeaker as it called for our contract facilitator to come to the only phone: "Bob Bradshaw, report to the office." This became a running joke, and we all had fun mimicking the tones and volume of the announcement, especially to Bob's face. Bob, however, never seemed to find it quite as amusing. It was a signature event, though, and Sam, to this day, can duplicate the announcement perfectly.

His strongest memory was one that eluded me altogether: the singular odor of the Oregon myrtlewood trees for which the town was named. Also known as California laurel or spice tree or just plain pepperwood, this was a tree so pungent that it inspired a bout of eloquence from sylvan naturalist Donald Culross Peattie in his book *A Natural History of Western Trees*: *"...always there is that pervading aroma, something like the true Baytree's, but much stronger, with a slight admixture of camphor and something peppery. One becomes aware of it after a few moments in a thick Laurel grove or under a great specimen, and the odor grows more, not less, insistent as you stay with it."* Over three decades later, Sam remembered that pleasing smell as if its source were in his hands. I envied him that.

Marmots were a playful bunch even if there weren't kids around, but Sam's presence in Myrtle Point encouraged new levels of frolic. I remember one damp evening with most of the crew jammed into a single motel room, lolling around like a pack of wolves. Someone inflated a balloon, and we started batting it around, trying to poke it back and forth across the room without letting it hit the floor. With a pretense of nonchalance, one of us would give the balloon a slap of the hand or a fist punch and we giggled and watched it swirl up and around in its unpredictable flight. We worked hard to follow our self-imposed rule of keeping the balloon afloat, which occasionally required a desperate lunge and cheers of encouragement. With collective passion, we swatted and punched the balloon for hours, sustaining it in the air as if the revolution depended on it.

We also planted a lot of trees. During the two months in Myrtle Point we covered hundreds of acres of clearcuts. Despite the new terrain, I found nothing remarkable about the planting. Slash, brush, broken tree debris, steep slopes, bags heavy with seedlings, sore backs, it was all the same. We drove from the motel up into the industrial forest every morning and drove back eight hours later in the waning light of the winter afternoons. We worked hard, but at a steady pace, without heroics, and planted good trees. It passed like a drizzly daydream; I barely remember the work.

One thing I do remember is the criticism/self-criticism meeting. So far, I'd escaped such gatherings, but, like most Marmot meetings, they were considered a mandatory part of collective life. I only remember one from Myrtle Point; if there were more, I've blocked them out. The idea came from Chinese Communist struggle sessions, utilized to great effect during the Cultural Revolution. As hippie disaffection in America transformed into political activism during the 70s, many Western radicals gravitated toward the examples set by the Chinese. After Stalin, the Soviets seemed morally bankrupt, and the iron-fisted gloom of the Soviet image wasn't attractive to the post-psychedelic crowd. The Chinese, on the other hand, represented a new way to do communism. Chairman Mao was anointed as a cool icon, people wore the caps, the red stars, and the Little Red Book became a worldwide bestseller with billions of copies in print.

The influence of Chinese Communism on the Left during the 60s through the 80s was considerable, lasting past the death of Mao until the Tiananmen Square massacre, when reality began to intrude on the fairy tale. During this era, many groups in the West tried to apply adaptations of struggle sessions to develop the "fighting capacity" of the radical movement. Mao said that "dust will accumulate if a room is not cleaned regularly" and "our comrades' minds and our Party's work may also collect dust, and also need sweeping and washing." Mao wanted a forum where "if we have shortcomings, we are not afraid to have them pointed out and criticized."

Struggle sessions in China, especially those conducted by the notorious Red Guards, were feared events of public humiliation. The goal was to berate and badger an individual accused of wrong thinking or wrongdoing, coercing him or her to make a confession through self-criticism. These confessions were staged in front of crowds who were encouraged to shout further accusations to propel the cleansing process. If the unlucky victim was reluctant, physical abuse could be applied for additional motivation. If the victim remained defiant or the persecutors lost patience, struggle sessions could end with executions on stage.

In Marmot, these ventures into the dialectics of self-criticism were called "crit/self-crit" and they resembled a demented form of group therapy more than revolutionary tempering. Unfortunately, putting people together in a group and encouraging them to criticize each other opens the door to cruelty and the darker sides of human behavior. Ideally, the criticism is aimed at improvement, even as Mao said, "It is necessary to analyze and criticize what was bad in the past with a scientific attitude so that work in the future will be done more carefully and done better." There is merit in this thinking; in systems theory it's called feedback, and we all claim to want it.

I was nervous when I walked into the yurt for my inaugural struggle session. I'd heard people muttering about these meetings, but I only had a vague notion of what to expect; at the time I knew nothing about the Cultural Revolution or Mao's prescriptions. I ignored that stuff and just did my organic anarchist thing, which was hard to define because it changed all the time depending on mood. I noticed right away that the chairs were set up in a circle, making it impossible to hide in the back. Indulging myself in wishful thinking, I selected a chair that seemed more obscure than the others. I perched lightly on the chair and fidgeted.

Soon Stan, the facilitator, opened the meeting. He started things off by criticizing himself for making a minor error in paperwork, the kind of thing that is inevitable if one does paperwork. After a minute of bland self-analysis, he launched into a longer judgment against a male collective member that he accused of sexist behavior. This individual was named and critiqued as Stan wielded a feminist vocabulary without mercy. Maybe the criticism was justified, but it was hard to tell from the meager details submerged in rhetoric. I cringed and sank as far as I could into the metal folding chair. The other people were silent; apparently, we were supposed to endure this sort of thing fearlessly so as to prop up our fighting capacity.

The next person offered another innocuous self-criticism, but being less zealous than Stan, she followed that with a critique of someone else that was so insignificant that it was hard to imagine that anyone even noticed the act in the first place. Another person went, and the pattern was established: lame self-abasement followed by toothless aspersions cast against the flaws of a hapless collective member. I was getting lulled into thinking that the meeting was more silliness than struggle when someone criticized me for being in a couple. They said that I made them feel "oppressed." I went beet red. I didn't realize that my relationship had been manufacturing counter-revolutionary dust in the mind of the collective. It's never taken much for me to fill with shame, and I felt it oozing out of every pore. What the hell was I supposed to do with that, anyway, renounce my ways and commit to proletarian promiscuity?

Then it was my turn. By that point, I was scared shitless. Not only uncomfortable with the idea of laying bare my soul to others, I also had no urge to share petty grievances. My mind raced with a litany of all the horrific deficits of my despicable personality, the endless sins and misdeeds of a sullied life, but I couldn't share those, the embarrassment would kill me. Instead, I stammered out something, anything. "I want to criticize myself for taking the last avocado for my own lunch, thereby depriving the cook of a chance to put it in the communal salad." I felt like a complete idiot. I followed that with an attempt to criticize somebody else, the safest person I could think of who wouldn't be likely to retaliate later. I babbled like a kid caught in the cookie jar, criticizing my innocent coworker. "Yeah, he... he took my personal hoedad out of the crummy, by mistake I'm sure, and used it all morning even though it was the only one with the big wad of duct tape on the butt of the handle, a habit I developed years ago so I could swing it one-handed, which worked pretty well as I'm sure he discovered but hey, I wanted that hoedad... I really did." I couldn't make myself arrive at a summation point, and gradually petered out. My turn was over. I paid no attention to anything after that, I was so consumed with replaying my comments and feelings and having my own crit/self-crit meeting in the middle of my head.

The meeting was horrible; I didn't like what it did to my friends. I can't imagine how terrifying these experiences were in China. I give credit to the communists for coming up with a truly insidious form of torture, the surgical application of peer pressure. Luckily, most Marmots didn't take these meetings seriously. I failed to detect any behavior changes after the meeting. I didn't stop being in a couple; frankly, I didn't give a shit if it was oppressive.

17

The Yaak Attack

A hamlet in the northwest corner of Montana bears the name Yaak, a Kootenai word meaning "arrow." A Marmot crew planted trees there a year before I joined the collective. Those who went to the Yaak job still raved about the beauty of that remote region, the broad skies and sweeping landscapes. The planting, however, had been brutal. In that country, clear-cuts regenerated quickly with a grass that covered the ground in sturdy mats. Although the work included easy walking on high, meadow-like ridges, when it came to scalping through the turf to open a planting spot, it took more than a few hoedad blows. The turf had to be chopped into bits or peeled off the soil by force. The work was slow and laborious. So many planters on that crew developed back pains that they considered it a badge of honor and made T-shirts with the phrase "I Survived the Yaak Attack." The shared adversity generated pride, but for many, Yaak was a bad name, and a place to be avoided at all costs.

When Marmot won another contract in Yaak, many members were running the other way. Not me, I poo-pooed the naysayers.

I'd been wanting to work in Montana for years; it was just one of those bigger-than-life places. Montana was still the Wild West, stuck in guns, glaciers, horseback glory, and Custer's Last Stand. Wiser heads urged me to join the other crew assigned to a contract in Darrington, Washington. But no, I was impossible, I begged to be sent to Montana. As is often the case when will gets its way, Darrington turned out to be a dream job, while Yaak became my own last stand.

It's hard to convey the unusual character of Montana. Its nickname of the "Big Sky" state is well deserved. Horizons are remote and as big as the world. Everything seems larger than it does anywhere else. Texans like to claim they are the biggest in all things, but that's only true for bullshit, where their reign is unchallenged. Montana feels clean, wide open, and brimming with possibility. Space and distance define every endeavor. Speed limits on Montana highways either don't exist or are whimsically enforced; otherwise, you'd never be able to get to the grocery store and back in the same day.

Montana culture reflects the frontier. Instead of taverns, you find liquor saloons occupying the oddest places. Celebrants could often be found lounging on the front porch of the Dirty Shame Saloon, one of two or three buildings in downtown Yaak. Out of exuberance, they might lean up against the wooden rails and fire handguns into the trees across the road, as if to punctuate their pithy remarks. Some people in the Montana outback opened saloons in their homes, which struck me as asking for trouble. While scouting contracts in a previous year with Gus and Lester, we'd stopped at a homestyle saloon. We sat on couches and easy chairs in the living room of the house, buying beers from the proprietor who kept them stored in a 55-gallon drum filled with ice. For a small fee we could use the shower. This enterprise had a hand-painted sign on the highway, advertising the saloon with an arrow pointing to the ranch house standing out in a large, open field. No other structures were in the vicinity. I've never seen this kind of thing anywhere else and certainly not in Texas.

The Marmot camp in Yaak occupied the same spot as last time, a couple of miles out of town on a marginal dirt road. When our caravan rolled to a stop after the eight-hour drive from Seattle, I stepped out of the truck and saw why people wanted to return. Set along the shore of a deep, quiet stream, the water ran so clear you could see every grain of gravel lining the bottom. Both banks were carpeted with lush, thick grass that extended along the valley as far as I could see. The wide trough of the valley plain merged into broad mountain flanks. Forests of pine, fir, and larch populated the slopes, climbing thousands of feet onto rolling ridges. Any moment you expected Paul Bunyan and a massive ox to ramble over the hills—that was the scale of the place. Aside from the road we used for access, no sign of human influence could be seen. The view took your breath away, and if it didn't, the sense of isolation did.

Everybody jumped to the task of making camp. Once the yurt and tents were set up, we built a sweat lodge ten paces from the shore of the stream. The lodge was used almost every day. Made from green saplings cut and bent into a curved frame, then covered with a heavy canvas tarp, it was just big enough for eight or nine bodies to sit around the circumference. Rocks heated in a fire pit were carried inside and placed in the center where they would glow deep red in the darkness. We went naked in the lodge. That may sound alluring but, in truth, once the temperature climbed to a thousand degrees, my thoughts were always focused on survival. After baking like potatoes in the dry heat, someone would pour water on the rocks, causing the stones to squeal and scald us in suffocating waves of fiery steam. I'd choke on the steam, lose my breath, and decide to just give up and die, every time. Then, somehow, like a miracle, a voice would start to sing. Usually, it was one of the women, and others joined in; they wove a beguiling round of lyrics about eagles circling the sun and other dreamy things. I didn't know how it was possible to sing because I thought I was finished, but the song went around and around and eventually I sang, too. A rarity, since I couldn't carry a tune. In the sweat, though, the group seemed to soar on the lovely voices twined together and who wouldn't want to be part of that? So, I sang and flew with the rest of them.

When the boiling and chanting were done, we rushed out of the lodge and jumped into the cold water of the stream. A few brisk splashes and then it was possible to flop down in the grass and for a moment feel completely balanced in all aspects of life and mind. We never pretended we were performing any kind of Native American ritual; it wasn't that sort of thing. It was a social sweat, a primitive technology of bathing unexcelled for scrubbing away the grime, the aches, and the petty moods.

I did my best to absorb and understand the implications of being a good collective member. True, I hated crit/self-crit and found some aspects of the collective process to be cumbersome or obtuse, but I loved being part of such an interesting group of people. After years of immersing myself in the macho world of production forestry, I especially enjoyed the opportunity to work with women. With the second wave of feminism at full throttle, the female cohort of Marmot tore straight into the nonsense of many habitual male perspectives. It could be embarrassing to witness, let alone be the object of these exposures, but there was something invigorating about it, too. Women in charge—I hadn't seen anything like it since I last lived with my mother. Of course, the women had foibles, too, but their contributions to the collective were crucial in making Marmot what it was. Among other things, it felt like a safe zone to me, opening the possibility that the people doing the job were more important than the job itself.

However, old habits die hard and often must die many deaths. Women comprised two-thirds of the Yaak Marmot crew and despite my new-found appreciation for women as coworkers, I still presumed that the physical demands of working in the Yaak would be a challenge for them. I'd been toiling alongside most of these women for a couple of years already and had seen how hard they went at it; I have no idea how I could entertain such an obsolete notion. Like I said, old habits. I'd been planting trees for ten years and as a former gunslinger, I think the presence of the women sometimes brought out a part of me that wanted to show off. By this time, I was comfortable with most of the people in the collective, a social threshold at which less-appealing traits tend to emerge. I abandoned all restraint and let myself inflate with hubris, determined to prove who was really the top-dog tree planter, a thought that had crossed no one else's mind.

So, I toiled and grunted my way through the work, pumping hubris. The contract was about half completed when I finally flew too close to the sun. It happened on a day when we were working along the top of a broad ridge with a view across the surrounding valleys and hills, a godlike overlook. The unit was free of slash and gentle in slope, which should have been ideal. But the tough Yaak grass owned the soil. Never mind the fucking grass, I was going to plant trees like the wind. As usual, I set off down the line in my best John Henry mode. Chopping and pounding at the ground with the hoedad, I tore away the grass, opening holes and tamping trees in demonic oblivion. I would show these Marmots how to plant trees. My goal was a thousand-tree day, a common benchmark for the Swinging Hoedads. The collective didn't reward this kind of scorekeeping because the contract was reimbursed by the acre and a quality plantation was more lucrative than personal tree counts. Besides, everyone in the collective was paid by the hour at the same rate. Individual glory didn't amount to much.

Before long I realized that I was being closely pursued by Maria and Margie, two Marmot veterans. Maria was tall, spent most of the year as a dancer, and had elegance; Margie was short, cheery, and giggled a lot. I considered them to be two of the loveliest women I knew and being around them made my knees weak. Both women grew up on farms in eastern Washington and they knew how to work. Indeed, they kept pace with me; I couldn't believe it. I charged along at top speed, but I couldn't lose them. I reached for overdrive. As much as I liked them, there was no fucking way I was going to let those two catch up. I streamlined every nuance of movement, dug down for total efficiency, threw all muscle groups into maximum effort, and jettisoned the remaining sanity. No matter, I couldn't outpace them.

What's more, when I snuck quick looks over my shoulder, I saw them gliding along in a slipstream of athletic ease as if they were out for a stroll. They were chatting with each other and laughing. Unbelievable. I had no intention of conceding, so I gritted my teeth and leaned into it, reaching for the final reserves. My lower back responded with a wrenching spasm of pain. The betrayal shocked me. My body let me down. There wasn't enough will in the world to power through the pain. I slowed the pace. I refused to call it a day, which would have been the sensible thing, but I had to let them pass. They went by with polite greetings, while I pretended to rearrange the trees in my bag. I spent the rest of the afternoon clunking along trying to keep up while my thoughts roiled in confusion. Margie and Maria, bless them, never taunted me, or bragged about kicking my ass. I appreciated that, but perhaps for them it had been enough to simply demonstrate their superiority on the job.

I sulked; the experience left me feeling old. Maybe it was time to stop tree planting, not only because my body hurt but also because I was a fool. Had it really taken me thirty-four years to learn that physical deeds didn't make the man? Had I even learned it yet? Probably not, since I kept on working through the pain, just another victim of the Yaak Attack.

My fascination with Montana ended on that day. I couldn't wait for the conclusion of the contract and the whole damn season. There wasn't much left, so I limped through work and counted the hours. I thought I could make it, finish with a semblance of honor. Of course, it wasn't going to be that straightforward. We heard that a Hoedad crew had been working in the vicinity and the Forest Service offered them an extra unit to plant, what was called a contract add-on. The add-on unit was enormous and the Hoedads wanted to combine forces with the Marmot crew to do it together. Hoedad crews loved this kind of cluster behavior and even had a name for it: "glom," an abbreviation of conglomerate. The Hoedads extolled the joys of their gloms, painting them as celebrations of human labor *en masse*. That sort of thing registered high on my skepticism meter. To me, a good number of people for a group is two. Up to six or seven is tolerable; beyond that I distrust the aggregate capacity for reason. I had learned to work with fifteen or more in Marmot crews, but it never struck me as entirely efficient. I also didn't like groups because crowds made me anxious. Call it a character flaw if you must. The proposed glom with the Hoedads would incorporate forty planters, an inconceivable number. The Marmot coordinators offered to chip in our fifteen crew members and an overall supervisor. Despite all my protests to the collective, I was appointed as the supervisor. I guess it made sense; I had the experience and was hurting too much to actually plant trees. Might as well run the show.

My first problem was to figure out a strategy so the bloated crew could plant trees without people continually blundering into each other. I went to look at the unit with a few others, including some of the folks from the Hoedads. Surprisingly, one of the leaders of the Hoedad crew was the same guy I'd encountered three years previously at the forest workers' conference who, without even talking to me and from across the room, had accused me of being a capitalist spy. He'd been annoying then, at a distance, and as I soon discovered, he was even more annoying up close.

The unit spanned most of a steep hillside and covered over a hundred acres. It'd been planted before, and a decent number of those trees survived. It didn't take an exact survey to see that it was a gravy unit, especially at the inflated price that'd been offered to the Hoedads by the Forest Service. The size of the unit suggested that the massive crew could be divided into sub-crews to work the ground in assigned sections. I figured it would take two full days or so with each work hour bringing in a significantly higher rate than usual. It seemed elementary: do the work, make the money.

However, Spybuster had his own notion. He fantasized that with such a large crew we could just run across the unit and finish it in one day. This thought got him high, and he couldn't stop talking about it. He was stoned on hubris, a condition I recognized all too well. His exhortations were succinct: "Come on! One day!" Frankly, I didn't get it. It was just another logging unit. The Forest Service wanted it planted, and planted right for a change, which we could do in fine style and with ample compensation. I figured it would be impossible to plant the unit in one day without missing spots and skipping over plantable ground. The Hoedad rep was having none of it. He didn't care about planting all the spots. He decided that even if we were penalized, which was bound to happen once the work was inspected, by completing the unit in one day we would be able to make a higher rate per hour than if we did it according to the contract specs. True, we'd make less money overall, but more per hour. He was infatuated with the hourly rate. It would set a Hoedad record or some nonsense. His insistence pissed me off. Aside from the obvious resemblance of this money-grubbing to the worst practices of capitalist forestry, and capitalism in general, our relationship with the Forest Service was involved. As the stewards of our public lands, they assumed that the trees would be planted. That was why they offered the add-on to the contract, not out of a need to purge government coffers. A romantic attachment to trees had drawn me into the planting business in the first place, and though my years of working in the industry substituted cynicism for most of the idealism, it still seemed important to reforest the butchered landscapes. Plus, I never liked the idea of cutting out on a good job and leaving money on the table.

We clashed over the philosophy. Still, an agreement was made to implement my basic planting strategy. "We'll see how it goes," he said, obviously unhappy.

Despite my sore back, I was determined to plant trees with everyone else and lead by example. That lasted for less than an hour. The Hoedad planters didn't seem to understand the idea of floating terrain in smaller teams. They marched up and down the slopes in disorganized clusters, using maximum effort to cover the ground. Growling, I abandoned the idea of planting and spent the time running back and forth on the unit, trying to facilitate my strategy. It took time to hike across half a mile of hillside, not to mention up or down a thousand feet of slope. No sooner did I trot off to redirect a wayward group, then I would see somebody else going astray and I'd have to hustle off across the unit. I tried to explain my ideas, blurting phrases while I gasped for breath. Clearly, things were out of control and my lofty plans were floating away in the Montana wind.

The *coup de grâce* came halfway through the day. Like a deranged cavalry commander leading the last charge against the redskins, my Hoedad nemesis emerged over a rise, waving his hoedad and screaming at everyone: "LET'S GO FOR IT!"

Before I could consider how to deal with this, he and a large troop stampeded down the slope, planting trees here and there, taking the widest possible swath so they could say they covered the ground, spacing requirements be damned. At that point there was nothing I could do. Trees got planted all over the place in such a slapdash way that it would be painstaking work to follow behind and try to fill in the missed spots. The swarm had spoken.

So, we finished the unit in one day and made a very high hourly rate, even after the inevitable and substantial penalties for sloppy work. I was furious. But it was over. And so was the season, thank god. I left Montana, went home, put away my hoedad, and never planted another commercial tree. It still bothers me, though. Going out with a pathetic whimper, like the poet said. That didn't seem right.

18

Cedar Rat Trials

By the end of the Yaak contract, I'd been planting trees for ten years. Many of the Marmot workers had been going just as long. We all felt the wear and tear of the job. Despite feeling worn out, I still needed to work, and I didn't know anything else. But we were crossing the threshold into our thirties, a time of physical reckoning, and everybody seemed slower. No matter how you viewed it, tree planting didn't look like a long-term career. Women and men thought about having kids, raising families, and cultivating the stability that eluded the nomadic worker. We had a good thing with the collective and wanted to continue, but with sustainability and a lot less dependence on those horrible planting and thinning contracts. Nobody in the group had a ready answer.

So, we did what we did best. We had a meeting and talked about it. The collective decided to spend a year researching alternate work opportunities, preferably ones that offered consistent, local employment and a minimum of travel. To that end, the collective advanced seed loans to any member that made a reasonable proposal for a new venture. A few members had already worked on a job clearing invasive plant species from ponds and other waterways, a task of keen interest to local land management agencies. The contract required the collection and destruction of the aquatic weed known as milfoil. The work involved a small, motorized barge piloted across the water while workers stood on the deck and scooped out milfoil strands with long-handled hooks. The milfoil was piled on deck, offloaded onto trucks, and taken where it could be burned or composted. I heard no favorable reports from workers engaged with this project. It was back-breaking work, hoisting the sopping wet weeds, and the tedium was unparalleled. Whenever it was announced at a meeting that more people were needed to harvest milfoil, like the others, I blanked my face and averted my eyes.

Always drawn to the visionary path, I embraced the spirit of new ideas. Unfortunately, I had more vision than sense and instead of scheming about adventures in plumbing, accounting, catering, or anything less physical yet still paying money and providing a career, I chose to pursue salvage logging. The reason for this (if reason is the right word) was that I loved carving up big trees with a chainsaw, no doubt a displacement for other immature fascinations. The previous year, between Marmot contracts, I'd worked on a cedar salvage job in Quinault. It wasn't lucrative but I had a blast and never bothered to analyze the economics.

I'd gotten in on the cedar job at the invitation of one of Gus's younger brothers who had worked with us in the Swinging Hoedads. At one time or another, Gus had hired most of his siblings (he had ten in all) and I enjoyed working with them. They were all a little peculiar, like Gus, but they made good companions. Fred was the youngest, brimming with energy and a sunny personality. His favorite pastime was fishing. Once during a trip to the Quinault area, while poking around for new trout holes, Fred drove down an overgrown logging road seeking access to one of the streams that drain those rainy woods. What he found was a car blocking the road. Curious, he walked to the vehicle and saw an adult woman tied and gagged in the back seat. Worried that the captors might be watching him, he quickly signaled to the woman, returned to his truck, and drove as fast as he could back to the nearest phone, a few miles away. The sheriff's team raced to the scene, picking Fred up on the way for guidance. When they got there, the police released the mostly unscathed woman and searched the vicinity. They arrested the kidnapper within hours; he was hardly a professional. The woman turned out to be the wife of a prominent logging contractor, and the perpetrator was a disgruntled former employee, which I suppose indicates something about how labor disputes are handled in the woods. As a reward for saving his wife, the logger gave Fred the cedar salvage rights to one of his recent clear-cuts, which also suggests something about the local definition of rewards.

The unit covered a vast swath of bottomland. Ancient logs of old growth cedar could be found under the stumps and debris if you were willing to scrounge for it. Fred was, he loved to scrounge. Fred was a cedar rat. That's what the loggers called us, because we were guys willing to dig in the dirt for wood. I didn't care; my parents had taught me to scrounge at the town dump during our family scavenger outings. As far as I reckoned, there was honor in salvage. Add that to my obsession with cedar and you could call me whatever you liked; just let me at it. Something about that wood induces an ecstasy in me, a cross-kingdom affinity that I can't explain without sounding like a mystic or a misfit. If you've inhaled the aroma of fresh-cut cedar, maybe you understand. Otherwise, just take my word for it: it's intoxicating.

Fred found another guy to work with us, Jake, an experienced cedar rat who knew the techniques and didn't mind sharing his know-how. Before it had been cleared, Fred's unit had featured a high percentage of mature Sitka spruce, and that species made up most of the logs taken from the show. Underneath the remaining spruce stumps lay cedar nurse logs that had slept in the ground for centuries. A nurse log develops when a tree falls onto the forest soil. Over time it builds up debris on the exposed surface and the bark decomposes. Seeds from surrounding trees fall onto the log or are sometimes carried there by squirrels and birds. A seed takes root in the debris and starts to grow. If it has enough nourishment and stability, it will send roots down around the log to find the soil of the forest floor. And the spruce will grow, developing a massive root system that grips the underlying nurse log like a giant fist. Linked to its forerunner, the spruce will find its way to maturity atop the previous generation. When Fred's unit was logged, some of the standing spruce trees were five feet in diameter and two hundred years old, still embracing the nurse logs of their youth.

The phenols that give red cedar its odor also preserve the wood against rot, resulting in extremely slow rates of decay. When a cedar tree hits the ground and evolves into a nurse log, it can fill that role for multiple generations of trees. Fred's unit was loaded with these veteran nurse logs, three-quarters buried in the soil and embellished with the stumps of their deceased foster children, the decapitated roots still gripping the trunks in futility. The mechanized logging show had no interest in buried logs—too much trouble. Just leave it for the cedar rats; they like digging in the trash. We accepted the challenge and cooked up a system to extricate the wood; a lot of prime shake and shingle blocks were at stake. Our system was labor-intensive yet simple: we carved away the straddling spruce roots until we could get a chain around one end of the cedar log. Then we severed the log at the other end, and by cranking a hand winch, ratchet by ratchet, we could extract the log like pulling a sword from a stone. Once resurrected to the daylight, the logs revealed their ancient beauty. We counted the rings of solid wood, subtracting an inch or two of rot on the exterior, and estimated that some of them may have sprouted a thousand years earlier. They'd lived a full cycle of old growth life before inclining back into the forest substrate.

The project fascinated me; it was ingenious, even though it resembled grave-robbing. After excavating and rendering these logs, we stacked the cut and split blocks into tight bundles about a quarter cord in size. We wrapped a heavy rope, looped at both ends, around each stack and cinched it tight. Because we worked separately, mining our own little fiefdoms, the loads ended up scattered here and there around the unit. When we had enough stacks, we hired a helicopter pilot to fly out to the show and move all the loads to the landing where we could pack them on a truck. The helicopter pilot was a marvel of precision and efficiency. We each waited alongside our stacks of cedar, eager for our turn. The pilot would fly straight at us dangling a 30-foot cable with a huge hook on the end. As he pulled up overhead, you were supposed to grab the hook when it swung forward and slip it into the loop on your sling. If you missed your grab, you might get clobbered with the gear. While you clipped the hook, the pilot rotated the ship above you, pointing himself back toward the landing. He lifted the wood, and you backed off as fast as you could without falling on your ass. A poor stacking job could result in an exploding bundle when the chopper picked it up, which is why you wanted to get the hell away. The ship tore off to the landing, where the pilot had a remote control on the hook and could release the load at the same time as he spun around to fly back to you for your next stack. He could complete three turns a minute this way, twenty seconds a load. It was unbelievable to watch, a man/machine athletic event.

While this went on, my heart synchronized to the rotor beat of the helicopter, *thump thump thump thump*. It was like being cranked on drugs: galvanized in hyperactive overdrive, a full-blown rush required for the jumping and dancing movements that had to be done to avoid getting creamed by the hook or the loads. An hour or so of this dramatic hauling was all it took to move a week's worth of cutting. By the time it ended, we were exhausted, but the blocks still had to be loaded on a big flatbed truck and taken to the mill. Otherwise, they represented a target for thievery, a common side occupation in logging country.

Fred and Jake focused on mining nurse logs across the middle of the unit, but I got side-tracked to the boundary where I discovered a recent blowdown. Windthrow is common on the margins after a clear-cut, understandable when you consider how the mutual shelter of the standing forest has suddenly been removed. At some point during a heavy storm, a giant cedar tree had toppled out of the tree line and fallen across a stream into the new unit, spanning fifty feet between both banks, ten feet above the water. It was the biggest tree in the vicinity, nearly eight feet in diameter and about 700 years old, full of old growth wood. Not, however, easy to get. The prime section of the log hung in space, far too massive to move with our hand tools. I wanted it, though, and wanted it badly. It would be like dismantling a god. Most cedar rats would have looked hard, shaken their heads and walked away, which was the effect it had on Fred and Jake. Tantalizing, yes, but not worth the effort. That left it all to me.

Crazed with wood lust, I mulled over the problem. The log couldn't be moved, so I'd render it in place. This involved walking cautiously to the middle of the span and ignoring the significant drop to the creek. I used the saw to make plunge cuts slicing straight down into the tree, burying the three-foot saw bar vertically and laterally. I used a sledge to pound in wedges and a rock bar to lever out shake blocks from the top. Once I removed the first section across the log, I worked within this notch, and it was easier to slice and pry adjacent sections. I labored back and forth along the trunk, sawing and prying. The shake blocks were enormous, and the wood was clear and tight-grained. Eventually, my efforts created a roughly level platform along the entire top of the log. The trunk was so massive that even after I took off a whole layer, three quarters of the log remained. It became my world.

I set up my sling loads right on the log for the helicopter. Lifting these slings required extra care, since I only had one line of retreat, and a restricted one at that. I kept at my project, skimming layer after layer of perfect wood, finally dropping the last section into the creek, and dragging it out in split lengths with the hand winch. There were so many technical aspects to the work that my total production went down, but I didn't care, the wood was amazing, like nothing else on the unit. The problems fascinated me, presenting challenges of access, tension, and angle. And yes, while I wrestled with this three-dimensional puzzle, I saw myself as a mythic character, a kind of mighty mite deconstructing the ancient grandfather tree as it slumbered over a creek of singing cascades. Should I have let it sleep? I told myself that eventually someone else would have gone after it, the prize was too great. Most of the trees like this were logged long ago or are now in protected groves, as they should be. I was pretty sure I'd never have a chance like this again. So, I took it.

After the big tree, I decided that cedar salvage logging would be a cool way to make money. I had little profit to show for my labor on Fred's unit, but I saw no reason for sober calculations. Big trees, big saws, and beautiful wood—I was hooked.

I got to know some specialty woodworkers, including a luthier, and learned about the market for odd cuts of wood, custom lengths, and other saleable items. Most cedar rats never thought outside the shake and shingle box. To me, it seemed a waste, channeling all that gorgeous wood into siding and roofing materials, when it looked so much better on guitars or cabinets. Plus, salvage had ethical appeal, cutting trees that were already dead—a way to harvest wood without killing, without clear-cutting, without leaving much impact on the land. It wasn't reforestation, but by that time I had revised my original perspective on forest management. Early on, I'd convinced myself that planting trees would rectify the vile destruction of the logging industry and therefore I could sleep at night as a minor hero. Over time, it had become obvious that tree planting was really a cover for the depredations of the logging interests. Not only that, it also served the purpose of providing more trees to massacre at a later date. Despite my original expectations for a career in noble deeds, it turned out that tree planting, thinning, road building, and logging were all part of the same show: the rapacious timber industry.

In the end a dark cloud of cynicism hung over my work. I knew that stewardship of the forest could be done in a responsible way. Harvesting wood is a viable human enterprise; it's been around for a long time. But it's evident that the clear-cutting of Gilgamesh and a massive scale of logging are not sustainable. As Derrick Jensen and George Draffan point out in their book *Strangely Like War*, "about three-quarters of the world's original forests have been cut." Forest looks like a renewable resource, but there's a limit to everything. Time frames for harvest need recalibration. The Hoedads in Oregon were starting to explore alternate forms of stewardship, becoming forest managers themselves, using selective cutting and horse logging techniques to revive the idea of sustainable woodlot management. In other words, going back to the time before the advent of corporate industrial forestry.

Small-scale, relatively low-tech logging appealed to me. So, with Marmot backing, I bid on a cedar salvage sale in the Skagit Valley. The sale didn't occupy a clear cut but lay amid mature forest. Five acres were marked off to include all the dead and down cedar on the hillside. I liked the idea of working among the standing trees, not cutting them down, not cleaning up after somebody else cut them down, but finding the scraps fallen from nature's table and putting them to use.

I won the sale because no one else bid on it. Still stoked from the mythic heroism of the Quinault tree, I discounted less glamorous influences, such as the myths of temptation, beguilement, and hubris. I'd performed what I thought was a careful inspection of the site before bidding, including walking around all the acreage surveying the available wood, mostly wind toppled trees, some old, some recent. There were no huge bonanza trees that could make or break salvage jobs. But there was cedar scattered all over the site, wonderful seductive cedar, and I wanted it. Had to have it. Not a good emotional state for competitive bidding. I was the kind of guy that brought a smile to the face of the car dealer as soon as I walked in the door.

When I received the award letter from the Forest Service, I drove straight to the office and handed over a check, courtesy of the collective. Now the wood was mine—well, in truth it belonged to Marmot, but that felt like the same thing. There was too much work to do by myself, so I recruited Dave. A collective stalwart, Dave was a hard worker who'd responded to my wild ravings about cedar salvage with curiosity rather than scorn or indifference. I couldn't have found a better companion; if he had reservations, he kept them to himself.

It didn't take long to find out why no one else had bid on the sale. The usable cedar turned out to be sparser than I had reckoned. Logs that looked promising on the outside turned out to be shattered on the inside (not uncommon when cedar trees fall to the ground). The easiest money in cedar salvage is in shake blocks. Two feet long, split into the widest chunks you can handle, blocks are light enough to throw around by hand and add up quickly when you take them to the mill. Good, old-growth shake blocks are in high demand. Unfortunately, the shattered logs provided few blocks big enough for the mill. It made more sense to split the wood into posts and rails for fences, a nice product but not in demand and not as lucrative. We ended up with a lot of fencing material.

The second problem turned out to be getting the wood to the road. The sale boundaries formed a rectangle and one of the long sides bordered the access road. Of course, most of the good wood lay at the top of the slope as far away from the road as you could get and still be within the boundary. We decided to use gravity to get the wood downhill. So, we installed a Rube Goldberg/cedar rat system of taut lines strung between trees—lines that would become elevated expressways for raw cedar products. Heavy gauge steel wire was tied to a tree next to the road, then hauled uphill and stretched around another tree with a hand winch. We pulled the wire so tight you could strum a note. At the upper end of the operation, cedar chunks were suspended from the wire with a couple of fencing staples hammered partway into the wood. The staples straddled the wire, the chunk hung from the staples, and a slight push sent the wood shooting down the line. When it hit the tree at the lower end, the staples popped off and the chunk fell to the ground. This sounds clever, and under some circumstances might work like a charm, but those were not our circumstances. Hammering in the staples was a pain, especially when you smashed your fingers; keeping enough tension in the wire was impossible, many chunks had to be herded down the line, and then chunks that slid freely would sometimes break apart into useless shards when they slammed into the tree at the bottom. Efficiency in a production system is measured by the amount of time spent on each unit. In our backwoods system we had to handle the blocks repeatedly from top to bottom; by the time they got onto a truck they had been handled too many times to pay off. It would have been simpler to carry them down one by one.

The wire system, our fundamental means of salvage, began to take on a malignant character. We kept trying to stretch it tighter to improve the downhill progress of the wood. One day it broke under the tension and a sharp end went snaking past my head like lightning, just grazing my scalp. I was careful to wear a helmet after that, not that a helmet would be any good at protecting the other 95% of my body from the whiplash of high velocity wire. More than once, I thought about an old friend of mine, killed in the woods when a high-tension logging cable snapped and caught him off guard, crushing his innards and flinging him to an instant death.

Even with all the fussing around, it didn't take long to log everything out of the sale. It was so much less than I had hoped. I took the liberty of expanding the boundaries, cutting additional dead wood that lurked over the line. Despite this improvisation, we still lost money on the project. I used all the proceeds to pay back Marmot the seed money and paid Dave a grim wage. My own earnings comprised a bunch of leftover cedar that I couldn't sell—just desserts, I suppose. And the notion that cedar salvage might provide a new career went straight on the shelf.

19

Party of the Last Part

The other attempts at new ventures yielded nothing. Collective members possessed diverse skills and interests, but outside of reforestation, there wasn't enough common ground. We had a couple of members who were excellent accountants, but no one suggested that we open a bookkeeping business or a tax factory like H&R Block. Maybe we should have, if we wanted stability, even though it would mean going back to school for many of us. We labored as blue-collar workers, industrial peasants really. The labor was simple, and anyone could do it. Sure, there were levels of sophistication to reforestation work, yet the basics could be learned in a few hours. Success derived mostly from physical effort and endurance, not to mention a willingness to get dirty. The thing is, Marmots weren't true peasants. We were too well-educated, too restless, and too ornery to take a place in the production line and call it a career.

The old-school tree planting contractors understood that the job required hard labor and not much else. The cooperative movement had muscled into their industry and claimed a share, but the old guard never went away. Instead of ceding the ground to the hippies and feminists, they redoubled their efforts by bringing in undocumented workers. We started hearing about van loads of Latinos busted on back roads deep within the National Forest. Immigration cops hauled them away in clusters, whole crews vanished in a moment. But these attempts at government control proved futile, just as they did in the food industry. Running crews of foreign labor was a lucrative operation: they worked harder than anybody else and for a lot less money. I saw plenty of them when I worked in the apple orchards; everybody knew they crossed the border, even the farmers admitted it. As long as they kept a low profile, which they did, no one said anything. I couldn't come anywhere near their production in the orchards, not even close. For them it was more than a job. It was sometimes the difference between life and death, not just for themselves, but for their entire families. For me, the stakes were never that dire.

Obviously, hard labor wasn't going to provide a future for Marmot. More than a few collective members had college degrees and wanted to work with their minds. Running the collective, with all the varied duties, certainly offered stimulating activities to challenge anybody's social and mental aptitudes. But the business asked everyone to perform the basic task: back-breaking labor. Over the years, members trickled away, enrolling in courses to develop careers in the trades or going back to school for advanced degrees and white-collar professions.

The conclusion seemed inevitable. Marmot didn't have a future. Like athletes, we could quit at the top of our game or drag out the demise, but no one wanted the pathetic drama of dissipation. We'd accumulated significant assets, including the fleet of vehicles and other useful hardware, we didn't owe money to anyone, and we had no commitments outside the group—why not fold the tent and cash out? We had a meeting, as always, talked it through, and decided to liquidate the assets, divide up the proceeds, and throw one final, kick-ass party. Miscellaneous hardware, too incidental to sell in batches to other companies, became the material of a members-only garage sale where we could buy our own stuff at bargain prices. That was a party by itself, full of chatter and nervous energy as we realized how near we were to the end. I walked away with a toolbox full of wrenches. The best five bucks I ever spent. I still have it, the only souvenir of my time as a socialist worker: a red toolbox.

A few sketchy details of the party remain with me, the rest washed away in a frenzy of cocaine and dancing. We rented a hall in Bellingham and a former Marmot brought his rock band to play endless New Wave hits until long past midnight. Marmots were avid for dance parties and all the energy that planted millions of trees got stomped out on the floor that night. I remember blurred hours of bouncing, shaking, and bass-driven rhythms as we all boogied like there was no tomorrow. Inevitably, the police arrived, and the band shut down and went home.

Several representatives from The Hoedads came to the party. They were grieving the loss of one of the oldest collectives in the tree planting community. They moped around with long faces, practically in tears. We ignored them and rocked on. I can understand the gloom of watching your comrades throw in the towel—like a betrayal of the revolution. But that was their perspective. I was proud of Marmot for recognizing that the premise of the organization wasn't sustainable. We searched for a viable basis to continue and the best answer we found required us to let it go. The organization had served a purpose, a lot of good work was done, people made money and developed skills, and now it was time for metamorphosis. Another cycle of life, pushing on to the next thing. Nothing wrong with that, and unavoidable, anyway.

And so, Marmot came to an end. The principles that formed the core of the collective didn't disappear, though. Over the years, whenever I heard about the activities of former Marmots, I recognized a meaningful continuity, an extension of the collective ideals, whether modest or grand. We may not have changed the world, but we changed ourselves. People formed families, maintained friendships, went back to school, pitched in for local and international causes, and stayed at it. In my own experiences I kept harkening back to Marmot's collective governance, especially when I had to deal with the petty tyrannies so common to the workplace. Plowing through the bureaucratic density of social service agencies, I sometimes found myself ranting at oppressed colleagues. "You don't have to put up with this shit in a worker-owned collective." That typically merited a blank stare or snort of disbelief. But I knew what I knew, and skepticism didn't change that. Like others, I'd taken away something of value, a belief that work could be more than a necessary evil, it could be the foundation of building a decent society. We'd shown there was a better way than just shutting up and kissing the boss's ass.

And of course, there were the trees. Scattered around the Pacific Northwest, those seedlings may have grown into a new forest. I hope they've woven their own fresh sylvan canopies; by now they'd be tall and sturdy. Or they may have become victims of climate or capitalism, struggling along with the rest of us for a place in the sun. I don't know; I haven't gone back to any of the units I planted. I don't remember where they are in the maze of the industrial forest and even if I did, it would take too much work to get there. Besides, I'm afraid there'd be nothing to find.

ACKNOWLEDGMENTS

Susan T. Landry encouraged me, as is her wont, in more ways than I can mention. She even edited the damn thing, though since I kept tinkering with it, deficits can't be attributed to her.

As usual, the Mechanic's Hall Casco Bay Writer's Project listened to recitations of the text without complaint. Their support and suggestions have helped me along the way.

A special thanks goes to Gus Plachta, the guy who initiated me into the tree planting cult and put up with me for years. A good friend and a stalwart companion in the fray.

I worked with numerous men and women over the course of my career as a tree planter. It's impossible for me to fairly express the value of their companionship. I've only been able to sketch the broadest outlines of the experience and its impact on me. For those who are not mentioned, or mentioned only in passing, consider yourselves lucky.

BIBLIOGRAPHY

Dietrich, William, *The Final Forest: The Battle for the Last Great Trees of the Pacific Northwest*, Penguin Books, New York 1992

Egan, Timothy, *The Good Rain: Across Time and Terrain in the Pacific Northwest*, Vintage Books, New York 1991

Harrison, Robert Pogue, *Forests: The Shadow of Civilization*, University of Chicago Press, Chicago 1992

Helle, Sophus, *Gilgamesh: A New Translation of the Ancient Epic with Essays on the Poem, its Past, and its Passion*, Yale University Press, New Haven 2021

Jensen, Derrick and Draffan, George, *Strangely Like War: The Global Assault on Forests*, Chelsea Green Publishing, White River Junction, Vermont 2003

Lonnrot, Elias, *Kalevala: The Epic of the Finnish People*, translated by Eino Friberg, Penguin Books, UK 2021

Mao Tse Tung, "Criticism and Self-Criticism", chapter 27 from *Quotations from Mao Tse Tung*, https://www.marxists.org/reference/archive/mao/works/red-book/ch27.htm

Mathews, Daniel, *Cascade-Olympic Natural History*, Raven Editions, Portland Audobon Society, Portland 1990

Marx, Karl, *Early Writings*, translated by Rodney Livingstone and Gregor Benton, Penguin Books, London 1992

Marx, Karl, *Capital: A Critique of Political Economy, Volume One,* translated by Ben Fowkes, Penguin Books, London 1990

Morgan, Murray, *The Last Wilderness,* University of Washington Press, Seattle 1980

Peattie, Donald Culross, *A Natural History of Western Trees,* Houghton Mifflin, Boston 1953

Snyder, Gary, *Back On The Fire: Essays,* Counterpoint, Berkeley 2007

Stewart, Hilary, *Cedar: Tree of Life to the Northwest Coast Indians,* Douglas & McIntyre, Vancouver 1984

Williams, Michael, *Deforesting the Earth: From Prehistory to Global Crisis,* University of Chicago Press, Chicago 2006

The author lives with his dear wife in a creaky old house on the coast of Maine. He worked for thirty-five years as a psychotherapist specializing in family therapy and wilderness-based therapy. Before that he planted hundreds of thousands of trees in the industrial forest of the Pacific Northwest. During those years he lived off the grid, built log cabins, learned how to lay stone, and survived numerous exploits of mountaineering, rock climbing, and backcountry skiing. He is the author of two novels: *Rhizome* (2021), winner of a Maine Literary Award, and *The Kraken Imaginary* (2022). His most recent book is a memoir, *Wasted Youth* (2024) about surviving the late 60s and early 70s. He has also published a collection of travel essays *Walking in Circles* (2023), and an ecopsychological essay, *Mirror of Beasts: Episodes of a Reflected Ecology* (2013). Website: www.wrightjamesm.com

The author in Yaak, Montana in the early 80s, near the end of his tree planting career.